SCHOLASTIC

The Primary Teacher's Guide to Speaking and Listening

• Key subject knowledge • Background information • Teaching tips •

Roger McDonald

SCHOLASTIC

Book End, Range Road, Witney, Oxfordshire, OX29 0YD
www.scholastic.co.uk

1 2 3 4 5 6 7 8 9   3 4 5 6 7 8 9 0 1 2

British Library Cataloguing-in-Publication Data
A catalogue record for this book is available from the British Library.

ISBN 978-1407-12797-2
Printed and bound by CPI Group (UK) Ltd, Croydon, CR0 4YY

Author
Roger McDonald

Editorial team
Rachel Morgan, Melissa Rugless, Sarah Sodhi, Alex Albrighton

Indexer
Eleanor Holme

Series Designers
Shelley Best and Sarah Garbett

Typesetters
Andrea Lewis, Shelley Best and Sarah Garbett

Icons
Tomek.gr

Acknowledgements

The publishers gratefully acknowledge permission to reproduce the following copyright material:

Faber & Faber for the use of an extract from 'The North Ship: Legend' from *The North Ship* by Philip Larkin. Poem © 1946, Philip Larkin. (1946, Fortune Press). **Hachette Children's Books** for the use of extracts from *The Orchard Book of Roman Myths* by Geraldine McCaughrean. Text © 1992, Geraldine McCaughrean (1992, Orchard Books). **United Agents** for the use of 'Poetics' from *Funky Chickens* by Benjamin Zephaniah. Poem © 1997, Benjamin Zephaniah (1997, Puffin).

Every effort has been made to trace copyright holders for the works reproduced in this book, and the publishers apologise for any inadvertent omissions.

Contents

Icon key

Information within this book is highlighted in the margins by a series of different icons. They are:

Subject facts
Key subject knowledge is clearly presented and explained in this section.

Why you need to know these facts
Provides justification for understanding the facts that have been explained in the previous section.

Vocabulary
A list of key words, terms and language relevant to the preceding section. Vocabulary entries appear in the glossary.

Amazing facts
Interesting snippets of background knowledge to share.

Common misconceptions
Identifies and corrects some of the common misconceptions and beliefs that may be held about the subject area.

Teaching ideas
Outlines practical teaching suggestions using the knowledge explained in the preceding section.

Speaking and listening

Before humans were able to read and write, the primary form of communication was through speaking and listening. Humans learned about themselves, their environment and the wider world through the stories they heard and the information they gave. Whether we consider the earliest 'grunt' or a rich and elaborative story, speaking and listening are at the heart of our very existence.

Consider the importance of talk by thinking about how many stories you have told this month, this week or even today. Our lives are littered with snapshots of stories we have told. These may be as simple as our journey to work, a lesson we have taught, a television programme we have watched or recounting a conversation we have had. Sometimes our stories become embellished with details and facts to interest the listener and, in time, bear less resemblance to the actual sequence of events.

The listener absorbs the words being spoken and reads the body language exhibited to react in an appropriate manner. Listening is an active process that requires concentration and continual processing of the information gathered through all of the senses. Meaning is made and knowledge is built upon through the speaking and listening we encounter each day. Therefore, it is crucial, with new technologies shifting the communication landscape, that we value the power, importance and essence of speaking and listening. We have to teach it explicitly to children to enable them to communicate with others openly and freely, forging new knowledge and understanding.

Purpose

This book will provide you with the subject knowledge you need to champion speaking and listening in your classroom. The important elements of speaking and listening are outlined and explained, each chapter providing succinct subject facts to inform you of the salient information. It is important, as a teacher, not only to know what you are teaching, but also why you are teaching it. Understanding and connecting with the background information will inform our knowledge and strengthen our teaching. This book will also provide you with a wealth of teaching ideas: some are detailed and refer to specific texts, but the majority are open-ended, with an expectation that the reader will apply their own professional judgement and experience to adapt the ideas to suit the situation.

Structure

The book is divided into five distinct chapters, which can be dipped into and read in any order. It might be considered curious that the phrase adopted through education systems is 'speaking and listening' rather than 'listening and speaking' as, arguably, listening is a skill of such importance that it deserves greater prominence.

Chapter 1 considers the various types of talk in the classroom, as well as offering advice for ground rules for effective talk and exploring the notion of constructive speaking. This is complemented by Chapter 2, which focuses on the art of storytelling, helping the reader to organise storytelling sessions, as well as to better understand the different features of traditional tales used in the classroom. Chapter 3 turns to the importance of listening and describes the difference between listening and hearing, as well as offering advice on different types of listening and how to achieve effective listening. This chapter also offers a wide range of listening games that can be used across the curriculum in order to develop active listening skills. Chapter 4 considers the power of drama to enable children to inhabit experiences previously unknown to them. It explains how a range of drama conventions can be used to develop speaking and listening, and offers detailed teaching ideas with reference to recommended texts. Finally, Chapter 5 looks at the concept of speaking and listening across the curriculum with reference to group discussion techniques.

Key concepts

There are three key concepts that form the basis of this book, although they may not always be explicit within the chapters.

They are outlined here to help you to understand the guidance implicit in many of the thoughts, activities and support given within this book.

- **Developing children's voices:** It is important that we celebrate and actively encourage the voices of the children we teach. This does not necessarily mean the spoken voice, although this book does focus on that, but also the written voice of the child. We need to help children to find their true voices – not the voices prescribed to them through dictating language choices, but the voices that echo the child's own background, experiences and passions. By enabling children to appreciate the art of speaking and listening and giving them opportunities to experience the trust, acknowledgement and acceptance associated with it, we can develop the true voice of each child.

- **Encouraging an emotional connection:** Finding an emotional connection to the elements of speaking and listening will enable children to respond with purpose, passion and empowerment. There is a range of texts referred to in this book that have been chosen as they inspire an emotional connection with the reader and listener, giving the opportunities for speaking and listening a greater degree of substance and meaning.

- **Working outside your comfort zone:** Many of the activities in this book will challenge not only the children but also the teacher. It can sometimes be perceived as difficult to enter into a class discussion, to have a philosophical debate or to explore characters' emotions through drama, but the result of pushing these boundaries in the classroom will undoubtedly result in a vibrant, interesting and meaningful curriculum for our children.

Teaching English is an exciting, ever-changing journey that we embark on with our children, facing the unexpected and journeying together through lands rich with adventure and vibrant experiences. Through this we will hone the skills of speaking and listening, which are grounded in well-selected texts combined with creativity and innovative ideas that will enrich the lives of the children we teach.

Speaking

While talking to some Year 6 children in a local school, they told me that one of the things they got in trouble for the most was talking. This could include talking to their friends in class, talking in assembly or talking inappropriately. It is, therefore, clear that children want to talk, have a desire to talk and, no matter how many times are asked not to talk, will continue to talk. The teacher's job is to harness that desire and need to talk, and allow them to play with words, hear the creative tune of words and experience the effect that words can have on the listener.

Types of talk

Subject facts

In the classroom, children use talk to: investigate, hypothesise, question, negotiate, argue, reason, justify, consider, compare, evaluate, confirm, reassure, clarify, select, modify, plan, narrate, describe, explain and evaluate new perceptions and understandings (Corden, 2002). There are many different types of talk that can be identified in the classroom depending on the context.

Private talk

Private talk is the internal voice that we all have – the voice that we do not always share openly, as it often reflects our true thoughts, feelings and attitudes at any given time. It enables us to plan, consider and reflect internally, using our personal memories as a base. This type of talk is ongoing and can be in total contrast to words we use and facial expressions we show. We can probably all remember times from our childhood when our mother was telling us off for something we considered a complete injustice. We may have been standing there taking the 'telling off', but our private voice would be working overtime!

Social talk

Social talk is important for us to be able to engage socially at various different levels, with a range of people from different backgrounds. From a child's perspective, there will be a difference between the social talk taking place with their peers and how they talk with the adults in their lives. Usually the difference is learned through watching others, evaluating responses and guidance from significant people in their lives.

Performance talk

Performance talk is predominantly well-rehearsed and structured. Its main purpose is to impress and influence the audience. Within school, children may be preparing a talk on the topic being studied, sharing out who will say which lines and practising before presenting to the rest of the class. The presence of an audience is vitally important, however big or small it may be.

Exploratory talk

Also called cognitive talk, exploratory talk highlights how talking and thinking are interrelated. This type of talk is not usually rehearsed, which is evident in the hesitation, repetition, pauses and constant reassessing of what has been spoken that all characterise this type of talk. Questions, both from the teacher and between the children, are an important element in exploratory talk. These could be categorised as:

- questions that find out what is already known (procedures, rules, imparting information)
- questions that shape understanding (extend thoughts and feelings, recount and elaborate on ideas, interpret meaning, inference)
- questions that challenge critical and creative thinking (using personal experiences to hypothesise and project).

Exploratory talk through dialogic teaching

Dialogic teaching involves extended periods of talk to move a child's thinking forward through the contribution, discussion and interpretation of a theme, story or idea. Children are encouraged to reflect on their own thinking by using effective questioning to build upon the answers and feedback appropriately. Active engagement is needed from the teacher who, through modelling and supporting, will enable children to explore and develop their understanding.

Why you need to know these facts

- Talk is one of the principal means of constructing meaning and understanding. Giving it prominence in the classroom and planning opportunities carefully will lead children to discover critical thinking. This is necessary, not only for learning in the classroom, but also for understanding and life survival.

- The dialogue between teachers and children is important as it has the potential to develop children's thought processes. When a question is posed by the teacher and an answer given, it is often the follow-up from the teacher that initiates deeper thinking. By responding with a comment or question, the teacher shows they have listened to the child and that they think their answer is valuable and important. In doing so, they encourage the child to make connections in their thinking.

- Using the curriculum to give children an awareness of the different types of talk and their characteristics will help them choose the most appropriate type for different situations. For example, the notion of 'private talk' can be studied when the internal thoughts of a character are made explicit in a drama; performance talk can help children feel the tunes of the words on their tongues as they recite tongue twisters or retell a learned story to the class.

- The guidance, advice and direction given by teachers enable children to broaden their use of language. For example, when listening or taking part in activities such as 'hot-seating', the teacher may work alongside a child to help them structure a question or provide an answer. This modelling and demonstrating is important as it gives children the structure they may need to imitate what they have seen and heard, leading them to internalise the language structure.

- Dialogic teaching that is interactive and allows for understanding to be built, shaped and possibly changed, is a powerful tool – it is at the heart of effective talk. See the Resources page at this end of this chapter for useful references for further reading.

Vocabulary

Dialogic teaching – teaching that moves children's learning forward.
Exploratory talk – talk that explores a theme, developing a greater understanding through the discussion initiated and developed by the teacher and children.
Performance talk – rehearsed and polished talk, often practised for an audience.
Private talk – conversations, usually by means of the internal voice, that are not shared openly.
Social talk – talk that usually takes place between peers and can be adapted depending on the audience.

Amazing facts

It is estimated that there are 6,909 distinct languages spoken in the world.

Teaching ideas

- Explore the notion of private talk with the class using a text such as *Misery Moo* by Jeanne Willis. Superbly suited to Key Stage 1, this book deals with the issue of friendship. In it we meet two characters who are best friends: a lamb who, for the majority of the story, looks on the positive side of life and a cow who, for the majority of the story, looks on the negative side.

Read the story to the point where it is clear that there may be some frustration from the lamb trying to convince his friend, the cow, not to be so miserable.

Stop reading the text and develop the notion of private talk by inviting two children to depict the lamb and the cow. They should deliver the external voice, which is heard within the text. Invite another two children to come and voice the private thoughts of the lamb and the cow. In the exchange, the children may come a little closer to understanding why the cow is so miserable. In the diagram below, the speech bubbles indicate the external voice of the characters, whereas the thought bubbles take us into the private thoughts of the characters which would not normally be shared openly.

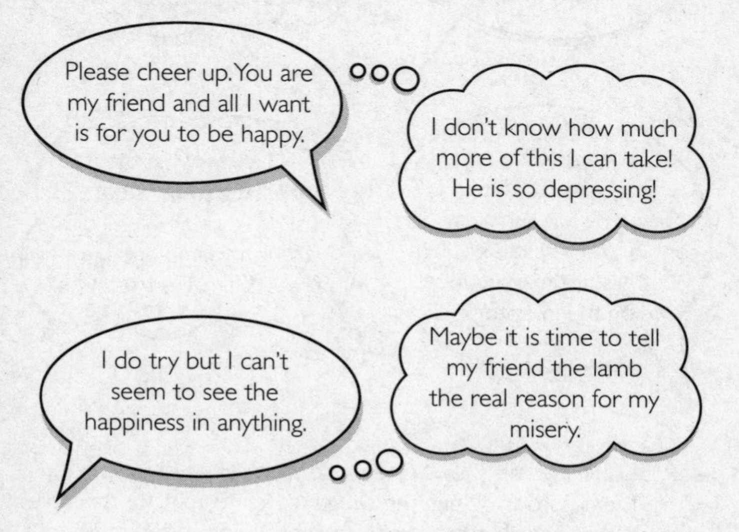

- Choose another text to explore the idea of private talk, such as *Out of the Ashes* by Michael Morpurgo, in which foot-and-mouth disease spreads across the countryside leading to the mass slaughter of animals. This book is more suited to upper Key Stage 2 due to the emotional nature of the text. Set out as a diary, the story recounts the experiences of Becky, her family and the animals.

There are many points where exploring the private thoughts of the characters would be enlightening, such as the highly emotive episode when Becky is hiding a lamb (Little Josh).

Read to this point and then role play the conversation between Becky and her mother. Becky will aim to protect the lamb, while knowing that she must hand him over. Her mother will be trying to discover the whereabouts of the lamb, while suspecting that Becky knows more than she is letting on. In each case, the external voice is in conflict with the internal voice.

- Popular television shows often lend themselves to adaptation within the classroom. Using the *Dragon's Den* format, for example, gives children the chance to rehearse and then present ideas to a panel of judges. This could be connected to a school council issue or children could be challenged to present 'Victorian inventions' for consideration – the idea is very versatile. Try using the *News at Ten* format to cross eras and decades, inviting children to report on the 'news' of their current topic. Recording them and watching back as a class adds value to the notion of performance talk.

- Myths and legends are the perfect vehicle for storytelling. Creating an atmospheric setting helps storytellers engage with their listeners, so encourage the children to work in small groups to choose a suitable area within the school grounds and build a 'camp' in which to tell their story. For example, a mysterious story could be told in a darkened area, perhaps using sheets and blankets to create a cave. Once the story has been planned and rehearsed, children could perform their story to small groups of children from other classes. Allowing the children to perform the same story more than once will help them to evaluate and change their performances accordingly.

- Poetry can also be used for performance talk. For this to be a performance rather than just a recitation, children should look at authorial meaning to then decide on tone, pitch, volume, body posture and actions. This could be part of a unit being taught or a regular 'poetry corner' feature, where children are invited to sign up when they have a poem that they would like to perform to the class.

- The availability of CBBC *Newsround* on television and online and the emergence of children's newspapers (such as *First News*) provide the perfect opportunity for teachers to plan for both social and exploratory talk. Encourage the children to watch CBBC *Newsround* either at home or online. Then ask them to gather in small groups to discuss open-ended questions designed to obtain their opinions and encourage them to justify their thinking. Not only will this allow the children to voice their opinions, but it also demands that they listen and respect the opinions and thoughts of others in their group.

- Newspaper clippings can also form the basis of many classroom debates, giving children the opportunity to explore arguments on both sides of a topic and allowing them to discuss and voice their own solutions to many contentious issues.

Encouraging constructive speaking

Subject facts

There is a great deal of research showing the link between being literate and the degree of control someone has over their life and environment. At the heart of literacy is spoken language, the ability to examine, question and negotiate. The development of constructive speaking in the classroom is, therefore, crucial to the development of the children we teach.

Organisation

There are a number of elements to consider when constructing opportunities for talk in the classroom. You will need to think about the groups you use – these could be, for example, random, gender or friendship groups. The layout of the room will also be important as you may want the groups to have specific talk areas with access to relevant resources to highlight the importance of the activity they are undertaking.

An environment for talk

A supportive yet challenging climate can lead to constructive classroom talk. You need to create an environment where children can be challenged, knowing that their thoughts, ideas and statements will be respected, in order to open up new areas of knowledge. Building an environment where children can work successfully outside their comfort zone takes time. Trust is a crucial element that needs to be fostered within the class (see next section on 'Effective ground rules for talk').

Creative talk

It could be argued that, for constructive conversations to be evident in the classroom, there needs to be creative context in which to embed them. Creative contexts, where unpredicted situations could lead to rich dialogue, do include some element of risk on the part of the teacher. Such contexts may include open-ended topics where the teacher and children explore new meanings and search for understanding in a collaborative way.

Words of possibility

In the previous section we looked at the types of talk. Within these are the words of possibility: words that encourage extended thinking and develop lines of enquiry. It may be useful to display such words in the classroom to encourage children to use them, not only to describe their thoughts, but also when responding to others. The importance of such language helps children to see that alternative ideas can be generated.

Wonder	Probably
Possibly	Might
Maybe	Could
I think	Because
Why	

Interthinking

It has been put forward that learning is a product of interthinking (Cremin and Myhill, 2012), meaning that the teacher and the child must use talk to create a figurative shared area for learning. Imagine the space as a highly motivated area where there is rich dialogue being modelled by the teacher and supporting the child to enable the building blocks of learning and understanding to be created.

Why you need to know these facts

- We all know how important groupings are in the classroom and how lessons can take different directions based on the groupings we use. It is worthwhile thinking about the themes being investigated and the outcomes envisaged. It may be that it is suitable to have random groups, but in some circumstances you may wish to use gender groups or friendship groups. This decision in itself can lead to increased discussion.

- The classroom environment needs to reflect the importance given to talk, showing it to be a crucial and fundamental part of the whole curriculum. Try inviting a colleague into your classroom to judge what is valued in your class. They may, for example, recognise reading as being important due to the inviting book area, displays of children's responses to reading, and children poring over books located in various places in the classroom. Would they also recognise talk as important?

- Using creativity is essential in creating truly constructive opportunities for talk. Creative, emotive and tense moments will propel children to solve problems through talk. This, of course, can then lead to artistic opportunities, such as writing, drawing and acting.

- Words of possibility can be used in all teaching. They help children to consider alternatives and justify their reasons. To some extent, the role of the teacher is to impart information and so deals in terms of certainties. But it is often useful to talk in terms of possibilities to develop learning, intrigue and interthinking, by asking children to consider the range of evidence and experience they have encountered before coming to a conclusion.

Vocabulary

Interthinking – using talk to build on other people's ideas, both constructively and critically.
Possibility thinking – considering a range of alternatives rather than just the existing idea or situation.

Teaching ideas

- The first days of a new class are crucial as this is when expectations are set. It is during this period that class rules governing behaviour and the workings of the class are discussed. Constructive discussions could include: 'What are our rights as members of this class?' and 'What are our responsibilities as members of this class?'

- Set up a weekly feature of 'talk back' time in the class, which could include a variety of stimuli. Identify the opportunities for constructive speaking for your class across the year and post a 'talk plan' on a display board.

- Discuss the concept of 'talk' with the class. Considering the area from a personal perspective, ask open-ended questions about whether the children consider themselves to be talkative. In groups, ask them to discuss a range of questions:
  - Who do you talk to most?
  - Who do you enjoy talking to?
  - What do you talk about the most?
  - What type of person is easier/harder to talk to?
  - What is the difference between talking to a friend and to your parents?
  - How can talking help us?
  - Can talking ever be a hindrance to us?

- To encourage self-confidence and self-esteem, and to promote 'talk' within the class, select a 'child of the week' to recognise and appreciate. Set up a poster with a photo of the chosen child. During carpet time, ask the class to highlight something positive that they have noticed about that particular child. Write the contributions onto the poster, which the child can then take home at the end of the week.

- Ask the children to stand centrally in the classroom while you read out two opposing statements. For example, *Children should be given homework* and *Children should never be given homework*, labelling each statement either A or B. The children should think quickly about which statement they support and why, moving to stand on one side of the classroom if they support A and the other side if they support B. Invite children to give their reasons for choosing that side.

Effective ground rules for talk

Subject facts

Constructive talk needs to be at the heart of classroom discussions, there should be ground rules to provide safety and security for the children. However, if the ground rules interfere with the constructive talk, then they, or the way they are implemented, will need to be reassessed.

The value of rules

It is important that children see the ground rules as criteria that enable them to share their thoughts, views and opinions in an open atmosphere where they are valued but open to challenge – the rules are not there to restrict them. Rules play a key role in our lives – to keep us safe, to uphold fairness and to encourage a degree of conformity. For example, we queue when waiting for a bus, rather than pushing and shoving our way to the front. When travelling in a car, we wear seat belts and observe the speed limit enforced for the safety of all road users.

Comfortable talking

Ground rules should enable comfortable talking – this does not mean that the subject matter will always be comfortable, but that all participants should feel comfortable in entering the conversation. It is useful to have in mind possible ground rules for comfortable talk when discussing them with the children. Children will have other ideas and also may not agree with some that you put forward. The ground rules can be thought of from scratch with the class, although Neil Mercer's excellent work on the *Thinking Together* programme includes a set of rules that can be used as a suitable starting point.

- Ground rules for exploratory talk:
  - Everyone in the group is encouraged to contribute.
  - Contributions are treated with respect.
  - Reasons are asked for.
  - Everyone is prepared to accept challenges.
  - Alternatives are discussed before a decision is taken.
  - All relevant information is shared.
  - The group seeks to reach agreement.

- A child-friendly version of ground rules for exploratory talk:
  - We will talk together to think about what to do.
  - We will share what we know with each other.
  - We will ask everyone to say what they think.
  - Everyone will listen carefully to others and consider what we hear.
  - We will give reasons for what we say.
  - We will pay attention and try to think of good ideas.

- We will decide what to do only when everyone has said all they want.
- We will try to agree about what we think.

Why you need to know these facts

- Talking in an open forum can be a daunting experience for some children. They are, in effect, opening their mind for others to hear their thoughts, views and assertions. In some cases, these may be opposite to other people's views. The ground rules are, therefore, important in order for children to understand that their views will be valued, both within and outside the classroom.

- Making connections between the ground rules for talk and rules across our lives will enable children to understand the importance of and the need for rules. By looking at situations where rules are lacking, both in the UK and across the world, children will come to the realisation not only that rules are necessary, but that they are key to safety and working together towards harmony.

- Children may be used to rules or situations within a school or class environment where talk is not encouraged. Not talking in assembly, lining up silently, silent reading and presentation-style teaching all discourage talk. Therefore, ground rules that encourage talk may take them some time to comprehend.

Vocabulary

Ground rules – rules that children feel comfortable with, allowing them to share ideas openly and confidently in the class.

Teaching ideas

- Discuss the concept of rules with your class. Ask them to think about their day so far – how many rules have they had to follow since they woke up this morning? Consider formal and informal rules – for example, at home there may be rules or expectations that are not explicit, whereas at school the rules may be displayed prominently. Discuss with the children the reasons for these differences.

- Consider the unwritten rules that are part of all our lives. What are the unwritten rules at a bus stop, at the supermarket, or in the cinema? Develop the discussion into looking at the reasons for these rules and how we learn them.

- Play a game that is popular with the class and has plenty of fixed rules. Without explaining what you are doing, fail to penalise any rule breaking. Once this has been noticed and before tempers become too frayed, stop the game and gauge their reactions. Ask: *Did you enjoy the game? Why or why not? Was it fun for some, but not for others? Why? Why do we need rules and a referee to enforce them?* Most sporting games would lend themselves to this activity: play football but do not stop the game if the ball goes off of the pitch; do not penalise children who run with the ball in netball; or allow some children to have a head start in athletics.

- Ask the children: *If you had to pick five rules for your school/society, what would they be?* Tell them to write down each of their rules on a separate slip of paper. Have a rubbish bin handy and ask children to throw away one of their rules. Which one is least important? Keep going until the children have only one rule left. Which one did they keep? Why? Compare the rules that the children kept to see if there are any similarities.

Resources

Recommended further reading

Jumpstart! Key Stage 2/3 Literacy Games by Pie Corbett (David Fulton) has a vast range of games to play relating to speaking and listening. The games can easily be adapted for subjects across the curriculum.

Teaching English Creatively by Teresa Cremin (Routledge) is an excellent text for teachers who are looking for a range of ideas for creative teaching. The chapters on developing speakers and listeners and on developing drama complement this book.

Literacy and Learning Through Talk: Strategies for the primary classroom by Roy Corden (OUP) is a good source of further information for those teachers wanting greater subject knowledge detail relating to talk in the classroom.

Teaching English, Language and Literacy by Dominic Wyse and Russell Jones (Routledge)

The Articulate Classroom: Talking and learning in the primary school by Prue Goodwin (David Fulton)

Exploring Talk in School edited by Neil Mercer and Steve Hodgkinson (Sage)

Writing Voices: Creating communities of writers by Teresa Cremin and Debra Myhill (Routledge) is a timely book, rooted in current research, which explores the role of talk in developing the writing voice of the children we teach.

Recommended children's texts

Misery Moo by Jeanne Willis and Tony Ross (Andersen Press)

Out of the Ashes by Michael Morpurgo (Macmillan Children's Books)

Storytelling

Chapter 2

We tell stories every day. These may be a mixture of anecdotes, explanations, jokes, reminiscences, embellished tales or recounts of stories previously heard; in effect we are all storytellers. This is not surprising as it is an art that is deeply embedded within our history and can be identified in cultures across the world. Stories enable us to express ourselves, make meaning of the world around us, and order our lives, as well as helping to give us an identity. Children encounter stories from a number of sources, including their family, friends, TV, computer games, internet, conversations and role play.

Talking about and telling stories

Subject facts

The power of storytelling

Storytelling is a social process of the sharing of tales by spoken word, creating a common bond between the teller and the audience. By immersing themselves in the storytelling culture, children can experience the creative interplay that builds between a storyteller and their audience. The intimacy of the situation fosters the creative tendencies of both the teller and the listener as part of a shared imaginative experience. The significance and intrinsic value of storytelling is extensive for a variety of reasons:

Stories have the power to bring communities together with a shared understanding – whether they are used to convey a message to a group of people, or because human emotions such as fear, happiness, guilt and embarrassment can be shared through the storytelling experience.

Moralistic stories try to teach people how to live their lives with a moral code in place, outlining what will happen if they do not follow this code. For example, the fable of 'The Wolf and the Crane' teaches that serving the wicked will not provide reward and we would be lucky, at times, to escape unharmed.

Pourquoi stories provide an understanding of the way in which the world works. Often, before scientists could explain natural phenomena, storytellers would be weaving tales together to help people make sense of the world around them.

Stories are also used to pass on knowledge from person to person, community to community and from one generation to the next. Before people could read and write, they passed on important information orally to ensure that it was not forgotten (although maybe slightly embellished!). Bible stories were initially passed on by word of mouth for many years before being written down. News of politics and great battles in history were also spread by word of mouth before the time of daily newspapers. For example, news of the Battle of Hastings in 1066 spread across the country through people telling stories of what they had seen and heard, long before the battle was immortalised through the depictions of the Bayeux Tapestry.

Personal stories

A powerful starting point for storytelling is to share personal experiences. This is a resource that grows day by day through our different encounters, either mundane or exciting. These stories are shared informally in the playground, on the way to school and with trusted friends, but they are also an excellent way to foster creativity as children revisit memories in the safe environment of the classroom. Through personal stories, children will have control of the tale, their unique tale, which they can shape through their choice of language, tone and fluency.

Traditional tales

Traditional tales belong to the oral tradition of storytelling – narratives that have been handed down by word of mouth through successive generations and across cultures. They are characterised by their use of repetition and rhythm, and tend to have themes that deal with life's important issues. The characters usually represent the archetypical opposites of good and evil, hero and villain, strong and weak, or wise and foolish.

Storytelling techniques

- **Voice:** Changing the pitch, tone and volume of the voice while telling a story will affect the listener, drawing them into the story and evoking a range of emotions, such as fear, intrigue, joy and injustice.

- **Gesture:** Hand movements can help children to remember parts of a story and can give them a model when retelling stories of their own. Facial gestures add a visual element to the retelling and help to paint a picture of each character in the children's minds.

- **Props:** A range of props can be used to add interest to the process of storytelling. These may be static props used to depict the story, such as displaying toy owls when telling *Owl Babies* by Martin Waddell and Patrick Benson (Walker Books), or moveable props used to show development in the story, such as finger puppets for 'The Three Little Pigs'.

- **Visuals:** Pictures can add interest and intrigue into the telling of a story. These may be images that depict a character or setting, or could simply be a colour, such as a blue card to indicate when children should join in with the communal voice: *The blue, blue sea wrestled and rolled.*

- **Music:** Sometimes traditional tales include a repeating rhyme, which can be sung to, and with, the children. It may be appropriate to have music playing quietly in the background throughout the story or you may use music to indicate the start or the end of the story.

Why you need to know these facts

- Traditional tales encourage children to join in with parts of the story, creating a communal voice and giving them experience of the flow and the rhythm of the text. For example, tales such as the popular European legend 'George and the Dragon' with memorable characters and a clear structure encourage both children and teachers to return to the text time after time, immersing themselves in the story further with each reading.

- It is important not to overlook the personal stories children come to school with. These form a valuable story bank that can be dipped into at any time. An intrinsic value will be placed on the stories told and a shared understanding and respect will be evident between teller and listener.

- Being able to adapt stories using a range of techniques can change the focus of the story as well as foster an atmosphere of creative involvement, offering children opportunities to explore the story in new ways. For example, quietly playing a mysterious piece of music while telling a suspense story can help to deepen children's concentration and draw them into the storytelling space.

- Knowing the various features of a story means that eventually children will start to play with oral devices within their own storytelling, such as metre, rhythm and repetition, and experiment with their tone of voice, the rhythm of words, as well as ideas, issues and meanings within their tales.

Vocabulary

Traditional tales – the umbrella term for myths, legends, parables, fables and fairy tales.

Amazing facts

In Anglo-Saxon England, storytellers were known as gleemen. Later, the term 'gleemen' was replaced by the Norman name 'minstrel'. Minstrels entertained their court by singing or reciting verse to musical accompaniment.

Teaching ideas

- Set up a storyteller's chair for the teacher and children to use. Drape a cloth over it to give it a special status. Invite the audience to gather around the storyteller's chair for readings and narratives.

- Organise an area in the classroom where children can access a range of traditional stories audibly. These could initially be stories on CDs or via the computer; this could be built upon by recording a bank of stories from the children.

- Invite the children to draw a 'story river' that depicts their experiences over a measure of time, such as a weekend or during a school holiday. Pictures and/or keywords can be used as prompts for each of the events, which can be as simple as watching TV, visiting the zoo or going to the seaside.

- In pairs, assign one child to be the listener and the other to be the storyteller. The listener says: *Could you tell me a little about…* and points to one of the pictures they find intriguing. The storyteller uses the picture or keyword as inspiration for a story. After a short amount of time, the children should swap roles.

- Using a story river, ask the children to pick an event that they think others may find interesting and practise telling the story in groups. Encourage them to embellish parts of the story, explaining that stories change over time, from one retelling to the next. Challenge the children to think of a title for their story that will entice others to find out more about it. Invite the listeners to discuss what they think would be a suitable title and agree it with the storyteller. Let children in the group retell either parts of the story or the whole story to each other, each time adding in some extra embellishment. At the end of the session ask the children to compare the last story with the first and to decide whether the title still applies.

- Set up a 'storytelling market'. Invite half the class to be storytellers, displaying the titles of their stories on cards at their market stall. The other half should be the listeners, who visit the market to choose which story they would like to hear. Discuss the children's reasons for choosing certain stories. The classroom or storytelling space will be buzzing with stories flowing through the air. This could be a great opportunity to invite parents or governors of the school to join in.

- Extension activities relating to personal and traditional tales:
  - Retell the tale from another viewpoint.
  - Modernise the tale.
  - Retell part of the tale and record.
  - Change the setting for the tale.
  - Intermix the characters from different tales.

Myths

Subject facts

The purpose of a myth was often to provide an explanation for the origins of a phenomenon. They were the stories through which people tried to make sense of their world and establish a moral code. The ancient myths arose out of religious rites, which offered people the chance to explain the spiritual side of life. Examples include the Ancient Greek and Norse myths and the great Hindu epics, such as the 'Mahabharata', a poem about how our world came into being, and the 'Ramayana', in which we follow the adventures of Lord Rama who is destined to battle with the demon Ravana.

Myths are usually set a long time ago and are often presented as events that actually took place. Often challenging to recount, because of their length and typically complex narrative structures, myths utilise strong themes to create a foundation for each tale. Classic themes include the journey of a hero with a quest, beauty and love, heroes and the supernatural, as well as the contrasts of good and evil, wise and foolish, mean and generous, and so on.

The Ancient Greek and Roman myths contain lessons reflecting the ethical codes of the societies, providing a guide as to how people should lead their lives and the consequences of not following the code. For example, in Ovid's story of 'Baucis and Philemon', this old couple are the only villagers to show kindness to the disguised gods, Jupiter and Mercury. Baucis and Philemon are rewarded for their hospitality, whereas the rest of the village is destroyed. The lesson of this myth is that our actions are always being observed and will be rewarded accordingly.

Language features

Myths are characterised by rich vocabulary, evoking vivid imagery, which is passed down through oral retelling over many generations. Imagery is used to help the reader or listener imagine the character, plot and setting by creating mental pictures. This can be aided using sound, touch, smell, taste and movement. For example in 'Romulus and Remus' their perilous journey is described as follows:

> *The basket was swept helter-skelter downstream until it snagged on tree roots and spun into a backwater where the wild creatures came to drink. A face loomed over the crying boys – a mask with yellow eyes and a mouthful of ravenous teeth.*

Similes are analogies or comparisons usually implied by using *like* or *as*, and are used in myths to liken unfamiliar objects, people or situations to those that the audience would already be familiar with. For example, in 'The Olympians', the thunder and lightning are compared to a knife and fork:

> *In the King's right hand he held, like knife and fork in readiness for a meal, a bolt of thunder and a flash of lightning.*

Description

Vivid descriptions of characters are used in myths to bring them to life for the listener and reader. For example, in 'Dreams of Destiny' Aeneas sees his wife trapped by fire:

> *He glimpsed her, too, paler than pale, waving to him from an upper window, beyond a curtain of fire.*

There are a range of interesting characters depicted in myths, often gifted with physical or intellectual powers. As well as heroes and supernatural beings, it is common to encounter talking animals, kings, sly villains, gods and goddesses. Dragons are popular mythical creatures, sparking the imaginations of both children and adults, they are a mixture of several creatures, presented slightly differently from country to country. The dragons of Ancient Egypt resemble serpents, whereas the dragons from China have horns like a stag and the scales of fish. Dragons from Indian myths are part elephant, whereas those in the West are depicted as fire- and smoke-breathing serpents.

Modern life

There is much evidence of these mythical characters in our everyday lives. For example, Nike shoes are named after the Greek goddess of victory, and Ajax floor cleaner is named after a Greek warrior who was a hero in the Trojan War.

Why you need to know these facts

- Some children may find it difficult to come up with storytelling ideas, however, by understanding some of the global themes used in myths, it is easier for children to plan stories to tell each other. For example, if they are using a wise character in their story, then they know that there should be a contrasting foolish character as well.

- Over time, children will become familiar with the structures of the stories associated with myths, which are often similar. This structure will then help scaffold their thoughts and enable them to develop the imagery through the vocabulary they use.

- The spoken language entices the reader or listener into the story, while images are being created in their minds. By understanding the language features used to do this, children will be able to incorporate them into their own retellings.

Vocabulary

Imagery – visually descriptive or figurative language appealing to one or more of the senses.
Simile – a figure of speech, comparing one thing with another thing of a different kind, using words such as *as* or *like*.
Structure – how the characters, build-up, events, dilemmas,

resolutions and endings are organised together to create a cohesive plot.
Theme – the underlying topic or recurring idea in a story.

Amazing facts

The oldest story ever written is thought to have been produced in about 2300BCE, which predates the Greek myths by more than 1000 years. It was written on clay tablets, the fragments of which are displayed in the British Museum. The tablets, called 'The Epic of Gilgamesh', originate from Ancient Sumeria in the Middle East and tell the adventures of the historical King of Uruk.

Teaching ideas

- Use a storyboard containing six strong but simple visual images to reinforce the sequence of events in a chosen myth. This picture summary provides both structure and a sequence to the retelling and will act as a memory prompt.

- Make wordless picture books of one of the myths chosen. These can be constructed in many ways, such as folding a piece of A4 paper to create eight boxes. Children can draw a picture in each box to depict the key elements of the myth.

- Gather a range of pictures of mythical beasts found within the stories shared with the children so far. Tell them that archaeologists have discovered a new drawing of a mythical creature from a cave wall. Invite the children to consider what it might look like, what powers it has and where it may come from. Ask the children to draw their creature and describe its attributes in pairs.

- Create a 'lucky dip' of myths. Put known or made-up titles of myths on cards with the children and post them in a traditional tale box. In pairs, invite one child to dip into the box and choose a title, which they then use to tell a tale to their partner.

- Use two dice: one with the names of myths on and the other numbered one to six. Let each child roll the first dice to give them the title of a myth to retell, and the second to indicate how many minutes they have to retell the myth. This could be developed by focusing on sections of a myth rather than starting from the beginning.

- Tell the children a story and invite the class to retell the it. They can pass the story around the class with the new storyteller taking up the story where the previous storyteller left off.

- With a colleague, get to know a bank of myths that you can tell your classes (see Resources section at the end of the chapter). Swap classes to tell stories so children experience a range of myths over a period of time. Make a display with the class showing where the myths originated. Add the children's own myths to the display.

- Over the course of a week, leave clues in your classroom and around the school, which will start to intrigue the children. The clues could include some fur, a large tooth and footprints going across the floor and tables.

On the day that you set up the footprints, gather the children together telling them that you found an old newspaper cutting about the beast of [your school/area]. Everyone thought that it was just a myth but this may be evidence of its real existence! Read the newspaper report to the children to give them some more information. Invite colleagues into the class in role as a journalist or an eyewitness and allow your class to 'hot-seat' them.

Ask the children to form a circle around a chair and invite them to step forward and show what they know so far by either saying *I know…*, *I think…*, or *I wonder…*. This will enable children to share their thinking and build on each other's knowledge.

As a whole class, start to put together ideas about the local myth ready to storyboard together as a shared writing time. From the shared storyboard, children can tell parts of the myth in pairs and embellish parts to interest the listener.

Choose a myth to explore through art, music and drama. Each group could depict the myth in one of the three mediums to then present in an assembly or on a storytelling session where parents are invited.

Legends

Subject facts

Like myths, legends can reveal the way people lived, what they believed, what was important to them, what they valued and what they were afraid of. The events in legends tend to seem more likely and less fictionalised than those in myths. Examples include the legends of King Arthur and the Holy Grail, the Greek legends of the Trojan War, and the legends surrounding Theseus and Jason.

Themes

Themes found in legends are common to the traditional tale genre. Popular themes include good versus evil, friend and foe, magic, strong versus weak, as well as a quest for something. They are important as they provide information about the way people lived and what was important to them.

Structure

Legends can be episodic, describing parts of a journey or events in a battle. Some include the entire life story of a hero, such as King Arthur, where each story tells a tale in its own right. The structure is commonly chronological and sequential.

Language features

Legends are characterised by rich evocative language, which is sometimes rhythmic and repetitive in nature and evokes a range of emotions. Imagery is effectively included by using similes and metaphors to create a visual impression in the reader's mind. Instead of comparing two things to each other, in the form of a simile, metaphors use a direct link between two things that are not usually seen as literally comparable.

Characters

Legends can include mythical beings, but characters are often more believable than those found in myths and have stronger connections to the real world of humans. The characteristics of individuals are often embellished or exaggerated, but legends often feature a hero or a respected person from a specific historical period, such as the legend of Robin Hood, which is set when Richard I was on the throne (1189–1199).

Myth versus legend

The distinction between and a myth and a legend often causes misunderstanding, which is why they are commonly referred to together. Legends are semi-true stories that have been passed down over generations, whereas myths are stories that aim to convey or justify a concept to the reader or listener. The key differences between myths and legends are shown in the following table.

Myths	Legends
Ancient stories rooted in sacred beliefs	Set in historical times and places
Main characters include deities and humans with extraordinary powers	Main characters are often humans
Stories take place before a historical time	Evolve around historical people
Seek to explain the origins of the world and the relationship humans have with it	Have passed down through the generations
Timeless stories	Often tales of a hero who goes on a seemingly impossible journey or quest
Stories often have important religious or social meaning	Most cultures have their own hero, such as Joan of Arc from France and Robin Hood from Britain

The legitimacy of some legends is still debated in the modern world and many people wonder if places such as Atlantis, objects such as the Holy Grail and creatures like the Loch Ness Monster are more than just the work of imagination.

Why you need to know these facts

- Myths and legends are similar in their nature so understanding the themes, structure, language features and characters will enable children to identify the differences between them.

- Knowledge about legends can help with an understanding of historical figures and can enable children to investigate the notion of fact and fiction. For example, by studying the legend of King Arthur, children can research his background and come up with arguments for and against his actual existence. A law court could be set up in the classroom with children presenting either 'evidence for' or 'evidence against' for the judge to weigh up.

- An understanding of similes and metaphors and the distinction between them is important for children to help them create images in the readers' and listeners' minds. Searching for similes and metaphors used in legends and displaying them prominently in the classroom could act as a support when children are telling their stories.

Vocabulary

Chronological – arranging or telling events in the order in which they occurred.
Metaphor – a method of describing something by suggesting that it is or has the qualities of something else.

Amazing facts

In the church at Zennor, Cornwall, there is a pew end that is carved with the figure of a mermaid. This reminds people of a local legend involving a chorister who had a beautiful singing voice. A mermaid fell in love with his voice and lured him into the sea to live with her. Although he has never been seen again, local people say that if you listen carefully his voice can still be heard above the noise of the waves crashing against the shore.

Common misconceptions

There is evidence to suggest that the Blue Willow pattern tale, which is illustrated on porcelain plates, is not Chinese in origin at all but actually the creation of porcelain producers in 18th- and 19th-century Britain. The popularity of this legend led to its use, either accidentally or deliberately, as a marketing tool for the plates.

Teaching ideas

- Make a class patchwork of traditional tales. Hexagon shapes can be cut from paper or cloth, on which children can put the title of their traditional tale on one side and a symbol to represent it on the other. You could use different base colours to represent each type of traditional tale – for example, all the legends may be on red cloth. Once the patchwork has been made, it can be used for retelling tales by asking children to choose a colour to focus on or you could role a dice onto the patchwork to see where it lands. As new tales are discovered or learned, they can be added on to the patchwork. Over the year it will show the extent of the children's knowledge about the range of stories they are familiar with.

- Discuss with the children different myths and legends about the sea. As part of your storytelling time, tell them about the Marie Celeste, which left New York heading to Italy in 1872, with eight crew, the captain, his wife and their daughter. The ship was sighted off the coast of Spain with no sign of life on board. The last note in the Captain's log was ten days previous and no one, to this day, knows what happened to them.

- Recount the mystery of the Bermuda Triangle, an area of water between Florida and Puerto Rico and Bermuda where more than 50 ships and planes have vanished. Read Philip Larkin's poem 'Legend' to the children. In the poem three ships set out for a long journey. The third ship, however, is in trouble:

But the third went wide and far
Into an unforgiving sea
Under a fire-spilling star,
And it was rigged for a long journey.

Explore with the children what might happen to the third ship. What could the legend of the third ship be today? Invite children to plan their story in groups ready to retell to the class as part of

- Using the idea from the Blue Willow pattern tale, which is depicted on china plates, invite children to choose one of the legends they know to represent on a paper plate. Start by telling the famous love story, set in China, which is about class and family duty. In the story, Koong Shee and her impoverished lover Chang are eventually transformed into immortal doves, who live forever above the landscape that represents their journey. Show the children the plate representing the story and challenge them, after retelling their chosen tale, to design their story plate. These plates will form a useful reminders for the children when retelling their tales.

- Working in pairs as 'teller and listener' partners, ask the children to choose a legend to retell. The first teller starts to retell the story (they may choose to use a story map to help them with the retelling). At the designated signal, such as a handclap or chime, the children swap roles with the listener now becoming the teller and continuing the story from that point. The challenge here is for the new teller to continue the story in the same style, including any extra elements that the first teller may have included.

- Make three large seeds from card, representing the basic structure of the story split into the beginning, middle and end. Put pictures on each seed, depicting the events at each point in the story, or a word bank to trigger mental images for the children. Explain that the children should hold the seeds to retell the legend and the seeds will grow, watered by the words of the retelling. This idea can be developed by the teacher telling the children in groups the beginning, middle and end of a legend. The children then join up in groups of three to retell the whole story.

Fables

Subject facts

A clear moral statement distinguishes a fable from other types of traditional tales. They often aim to teach the reader or listener a lesson for life and are characterised by a fictitious plot and simple narrative. The most common of these are by Aesop and La Fontaine.

Themes

The themes are similar to those found across the other traditional tales, however the purpose in fables is to teach the reader or listener a lesson regarding how to live their lives. Fables are clearly fictitious and do not pretend to be based on fact, focusing instead on providing a frame for the moral premise.

Fables have been used to teach morals and values across generations. The principles and messages contained in the fables are clear, guiding children to develop moral reasoning and, in turn, an understanding of their own behaviour. Examples of the morals taught in some fables are shown in the following table.

Fable	Moral
The Ant and the Grasshopper	There is a time to work and a time to play
The Fox and the Stork	If you trick others you may be tricked yourself
The Boy Who Cried Wolf	Liars are not believed, even when they tell the truth
The Fox and the Crow	Never trust a flatterer

Structure

There is usually a very simple structure associated with fables, making them easier to retell than some of the other traditional tales. This usually consists of an opening, a problem or dilemma, and then the resolution. Fables are short and usually contain two characters, who meet, go on a short journey of discovery and then go their separate ways. The main character is often used in the title, such as 'The Boy Who Cried Wolf' and 'The Sick Lion'. They also sometimes feature animals who talk like humans.

The simple structure of fables can be revealed in the classic tale of 'The Hare and the Tortoise':

Beginning	The hare boasts about never being beaten in a race. The tortoise challenges the hare to a race.
Problem	The hare is so confident he stops to rest and falls asleep.
Resolution	The determined tortoise passes the sleeping hare and wins the race.
Moral	Never give up as determination can win the day.

Language features

There is little description in fables as the events are key to teaching the lesson, rather than the imagery. Similarly, there is little description of the characters because it is their actions that are the focus, rather than building a relationship or familiarity between the characters and the audience.

Connectives

Connectives are words that connect phrases, clauses or individual words. Common examples of connectives include *after*, *when*, *also*, *in addition* and *despite*. Connectives can be used in fables to show the cause and effect of events within the story. Cause and effect connectives include *because*, *so*, *therefore*, *thus* and *consequently*.

Temporal connectives

These are also called 'time connectives' and feature in fables to hold the narrative together and give it a chronological shape: *One morning…*, *As he was…*, *First he saw…*, *Then he saw…*, *When winter came…*, *And then the grasshopper understood…*

Why you need to know these facts

- Being familiar with the features of fables will help children to use and adapt these features and structure, reworking characters and developing their own storylines.

- Children will quickly learn the simple structure in fables, appreciating the predictable narrative and applying it to their own speaking and writing. For example, the fable 'The Wind and the Sun' follows a simple and predictable pattern:
  - **Beginning:** The wind and the sun are having an argument about who is stronger. They see a man and decide that the winner will be the one who manages to make the man take off his coat.
  - **Pattern:** The two characters are very competitive. A challenge is set.
  - **Middle:** The wind starts by blowing furiously at the man, resulting in him pulling his coat closer around him. It is then the sun's turn. The sun beams light at the man, bathing him in warmth.
  - **Pattern:** The two characters compete to show who is strongest.
  - **Ending:** The man preferred the warmth to the harsh wind and so takes off his coat.
  - **Pattern:** One character overcomes the other.
  - **Moral:** You can accomplish more with kindness than with force.

- Fables help to extend children's moral development. Due to the nature of the morals being taught, children will be challenged to think critically about ethical issues and can be encouraged to relate this to their own values. Fables could be used in assembly and also in PSHE lessons or circle time to reinforce various moral codes of conduct.

- Focusing on metaphors can help children understand the figurative language being used. This increases higher-level thinking as they interpret what is meant by the language to develop their inference and deduction skills.

Vocabulary

Connective – words that connect phrases, clauses or individual words.
Fable – a fictitious story or tale, intended to instruct some useful truth or to amuse.
Moral – a lesson that is taught through a fictitious story.
Temporal connective – a connective that links things in time, such as *after this, later* and *then*.

Amazing facts

One of the most famous collections of fables was put together by Aesop. It is believed that Aesop was a slave and storyteller who lived in Ancient Greece between 620BC and 560BC.

Common misconceptions

Young children in particular tend to worry about 'getting the story right' or 'remembering it all'. Regular retelling of tales supported by discussion can help children to realise that this is not an essential part of the exercise.

Teaching ideas

- Have regular storytelling sessions in class using fables. Because they are short and have a simple structure, they can be easier to remember. This will ensure that children are given opportunities to actively listen and respond to the fables and become familiar with their structure, cadence and conventions.

- Create board games based on one of the children's favourite fables, ensuring all the choices given for each particular game relate to the moral of the fable.

- Story maps are an excellent way of remembering a fable. Story maps are drawn by recording the geographical locations in the tale and plotting the central pathway taken by the character. These can be used for all traditional tales, but would probably be simplest when based on a fable. The map depicts the path of the action and it can include any significant words or phrases relevant to the tale. Let the children work in a group to share their ideas about the physical and structural features of the tale.

- Read a fable such as 'The Oak and the Reeds'. In this fable, the mighty oak tree stands strong amongst a sea of reeds. Teasingly, the oak tells the reeds that they are puny. Soon after, a great wind comes and the oak tree snaps and crashes to the ground. One quiet reed tells the oak tree that he fought against the wind and broke, whereas the reeds bent with the wind and survived. The moral of the fable is that it is sometimes better to bend than to break. Use pictures to depict the sections of the story and encourage the children to retell it. After talking to the children about the moral of the story, ask them whether they can replace the characters with two different ones. From this, they can then tell their own versions of the fable.

- Work with the children to making a story mountain to help them retell a tale. Fables are a good starting point if children have not used a story mountain before, as they have a simple structure, and can be used as the base for more complicated mountains. The basic idea is to use the shape of a mountain to depict the different parts of the story. The bottom of the mountain will be the opening. The peak of the mountain will be the dilemma and the bottom of the mountain will be the resolution. Written within the mountain can be the moral. Give the children cards with each part of the story on and ask them to place them on the class mountain, before making mini mountains of their own for other fables they know.

Fairy tales

Subject facts

Fairy tales were passed down orally to amuse and to convey cultural information that influences behaviour, such as where it is safe to travel and to be home before dark. They are derived from folk tales, some of which were adapted by writers such as Hans Christian Anderson, Oscar Wilde and John Ruskin. Examples include the many written tales originally recorded by historians and scholars, such as 'Rapunzel', 'Snow White' and 'Hansel and Gretel' published by the Brothers Grimm.

Themes

Fairy-tale themes are similar to those found across the genre of traditional tales. Fairy tales are also known as wonder tales or *märchen* (the German word for fairy tales) and, as such, they include magical themes as well as good and evil, safe and dangerous, weak and strong, and beauty and ugliness. They are fictional stories, often in timeless, generic, unspecified settings. They function to entertain, inspire and enlighten the audience.

The themes are different from the morals of fables as each tale also teaches us a lesson. For example, in 'Hansel and Gretel' the theme could be considered to be one of 'safe and dangerous' but we also learn the moral that we should not take what isn't ours and, possibly, not eat too many sweets!

Fairy tale	Theme
The Princess and the Pea	Character is put to a test
Snow White	Jealousy of a character's beauty and goodness
Hansel and Gretel	Evil is punished
Beauty and the Beast	Love story based on beauty beyond appearance
Cinderella	Rags to riches
Sleeping Beauty	True love conquers all

Structure

Fairy tales often have repetitive, sequential and accumulating patterns. Starting with a formulaic opening, these tales are often identified by phrases such as *Once upon a time…*, *A long time ago…* or *In a land far, far away…*. Specific structures vary but can involve characters being banished from their land and having to fulfil a journey or quest in order to return. The hero of the story has to overcome adversaries, which could be a witch, a monster, an ogre or an evil fairy. We can look at the structure of specific fairy tales in relation to a story mountain. A simple story mountain shows the different parts of a story, from the beginning at the bottom of the mountain, to the middle at the top of the mountain, and the ending down the other side of the mountain.

Language features

Fairy tales often use archaic language features, indicating that they are telling the tale of another place 'far, far away'; the unfamiliar language sets the story out of reach for the listener. For example, in the opening of 'Hansel and Gretel' many archaic words and phrases can be identified:

> *By a great forest dwelt a poor woodcutter with his wife and his two children. The boy was called Hansel and the girl Gretel. He had little to bite and to break, and once when great dearth fell on the land, he could no longer procure even daily bread.*

It is worth reading the opening a couple of times and considering the effect it has on you. They are useful passages to explore the skills of inference and deduction with children.

Phrases or expressions are repeated for emphasis or for theatrical effect. For example, in 'Jack and the Beanstalk' the giant's refrain of *"Fee fi fo fum, I smell the blood of an Englishman"* is enjoyable to repeat and recreate in the giant's booming voice. In the story of 'The Three Little Pigs', the famous refrain of the wolf, as he threatens to 'Huff and puff and blow the house down', again encourages us to join in with the storyteller.

In many of the fairy tales, a series of three objects, events or actions can be identified. These trinities can help the teller to remember the story and they build the anticipation for the listener as they listen out for the sequence. Examples include Aladdin's three wishes and Jack retrieving three items from the giant – the golden coins, the golden hen and the golden harp.

Characters

Fairy-tale characters are interesting, believable characters that, as a reader, we develop empathy for. Within each fairy tale we can come into contact with a range of characters including heroes, villains, kings, queens, knights, farmers, wise women and hardworking people looking for a better life.

Modern fairy tales

It is the very nature of fairy tales that they have been retold and evolved over time. It is thought that in the original tale of 'Cinderella' the stepsisters cut off their heels in order to fit their feet into the glass slipper; then at end of the story, their eyes were pecked out by birds as punishment. These details, as with many other fairy tales, have changed over time to make them more suitable for sharing with children.

Therefore, it stands to reason that these tales will continue to change over time and into the future. In some cases this has included twisting tales and mixing characters within them. For example, 'The Three Little Pigs' has been adapted into, amongst other titles, *The True Story of the Three Little Pigs* by Jon Scieszka, as well as *The Three Little Wolves and the Big Bad Pig* by Eugene Trivizas.

Animated film adaptations of the fairy-tale genre have included playful reworkings, including the use of humour in *Shrek* and in the interpretation of the Brothers Grimm tale of 'Rapunzel' in the 2010 film *Tangled*.

Why you need to know these facts

- The particular story patterns of fairy tales mean that they are usually memorable and predictable and so they are exceptionally suitable for young children to retell.

- The repetitive pattern of some of the fairy tales moves some tales on, while also providing breathing spaces within the narrative, during which the audience chant the refrain and simultaneously predict and reflect on the story.

- It is important to be able to identify the language features found within fairy tales as this will be a feature in the retellings of the tales. Children will push themselves to use archaic language, possibly choosing words that do not entirely fit, but demonstrating an understanding of the style that is required.

- Some may consider fairy tales to be suitable for younger children, in fact, due to their historic nature, many of the original tales would not be suitable for a primary classroom. Some of the modern tales may interest the children because of their humour and slightly subversive nature.

Vocabulary

Archaic language – language originating from the past that is not currently used in daily life.
Repetitive language – language that reoccurs throughout the story, often encouraging a communal voice.
Rhythmic language – language that forms a recurring beat or cadence, used to make the story more memorable.

Amazing facts

The Arabian Nights stories are some of the earliest-known fairy tales: 'Aladdin', 'Ali Baba' and 'Sinbad the Sailor' have been told across Persia, Arabia, India and Asia, and have now become part of Western folklore.

Teaching ideas

- Emotion graphs work well to show how the emotions of a character change over time. Within a fairy tale it is usual for the main characters to experience emotional extremes. For example, contrasting Snow White's emotions with her stepmother's polarised emotional states provides intriguing material for discussion.

- Ask children to put together a storytelling bag for their chosen fairy tale to tell at home. The bag could contain simple props, puppets and artefacts used to prompt retellings at home and to provide visual memory aids for the children.

- Pairs could be asked to select a memory from one of the fairy tales they have just heard and to 'freeze' it as a visual image in their minds to share with a story partner. In this instance, each child retells only a section of the tale, starting just before the moment they froze the tale in their mind and finishing just after. This reduces the length of the storytelling and encourages children to focus on the detail of one section of the tale.

- Make a class basket filled with cards with the names of fairy-tale characters on. Model the activity for your children by picking a card at random and inviting the class to guess who it is using the description you provide. Over time, discuss with the class the role of the person describing the character; talk about how you tease the audience with general facts first, which could fit a variety of characters, before releasing specific information about the character.

- Make a story mountain displaying the main events in the story. Children can then plot the events of the story on the mountain showing their understanding of story structure. For example, for the story of 'Cinderella' either give the children the main events or ask them in groups to write down the main elements of the story. In the example below, the main events are shown in a random order as they would be presented to children in the class to enable them to discuss the story order and structure. Encourage the children to use their story mountain when retelling the story of 'Cinderella', whether in pairs or as a group.

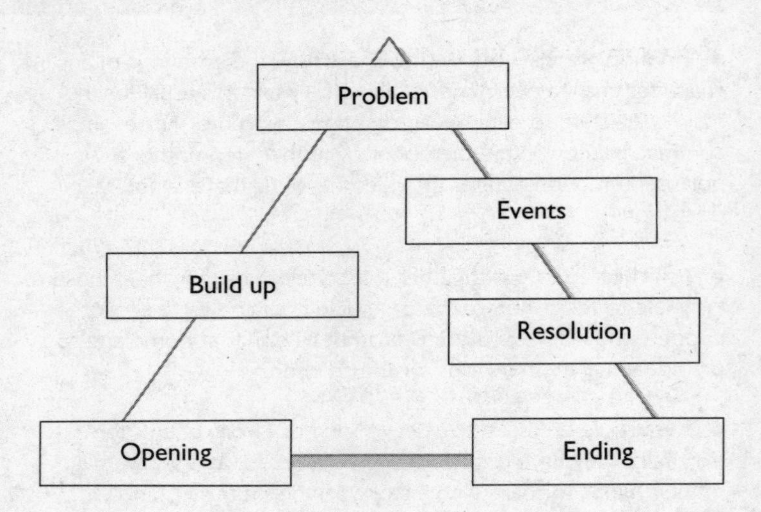

Cinderella's stepsisters get ready to go to the ball.

An invitation arrives from the palace inviting the sisters to the ball.

The ugly stepsisters attempt to fit their feet into the glass slipper.

Cinderella marries the handsome prince.

Cinderella arrives at the palace and dances with the prince.

Cinderella is treated badly by her stepsisters and is forced to clean and wash the floors.

A fairy godmother appears and grants Cinderella three wishes.

Cinderella gets a horse-drawn carriage, a beautiful dress and glass slippers.

The clock strikes midnight. Cinderella leaves but loses her glass slipper.

The prince announces he will marry whoever fits the slipper.

The prince and Cinderella live happily ever after.

Resources

Recommended further reading

Tales, Tellers and Texts by Gabrielle Cliff Hodges, Mary Jane Drummond and Morag Styles (Cassell Education)

Planning Creative Literacy Lessons by Andrew Lambirth (David Fulton) is an extremely useful text covering a wide range of classroom experiences. The chapter on Greek mythology and the chapter about traditional tales and storytelling are particularly pertinent to this book.

Jumpstart! Storymaking: Games and activities for ages 7–12 by Pie Corbett (David Fulton)

Recommended children's texts

The True Story of the Three Little Pigs by Jon Scieszka (Puffin)

The Three Little Wolves and the Big Bad Pig by Eugene Trivizas (Egmont Books)

Listening

Chapter 3

Hearing is something we possibly take for granted. Most of us can actively control whether we speak or not, but it is harder to control whether we hear. To stop ourselves hearing we would need to physically move ourselves away from an area or cover our ears. Apart from that we do not have control over the sound waves towards us. So why, in the classroom, do we sometimes assume that children are not listening to what we are saying? We first need to investigate what listening actually is.

Listening and hearing

Subject facts

Although we sometimes use the terms 'hearing' and 'listening' interchangeably, they actually mean two different things. The difference is important to understand, as most people have the ability to hear but not always to listen.

We know that sound waves are all around us and enter our ears constantly. As I write this I can hear the hum of an aeroplane, the beeping of a reversing horn and the chatter of talk from outside the window. I cannot easily control whether those waves enter my ears or not. However, we also know that we sometimes say *he's just not listening*, *she has selective hearing*, or *he never listens to what I've got to say*.

Hearing, unless you are hearing impaired, happens constantly and is generally out of your control. Listening, on the other hand, is something we choose to do. When we listen, we have to actively concentrate and our brain needs to process the sound waves and act on them. Therefore, it is the practice of listening that leads to learning.

The skills of listening

Listening is vital to learning. Before people were able to read and write, the primary method of communicating was by speaking and listening. Through listening, people were able to receive messages and obtain information.

There are nine identifiable skills needed when listening:

- **Predicting and anticipating:** This is a listener-based skill whereby the listener uses their background knowledge and understanding of the situation to predict future aspects of what they are listening to. This could be, for example, a child being told off by one of his parents for breaking a glass. Using the knowledge he has of the situation (maybe having experienced it before) and the predictability of what is being said, he may know that he is about to be sent to his room.

  Within the classroom, children may predict in their heads what the dilemma will be in the story that you are reading to them. They will be able to do this if they have had a range of experiences listening to a similar genre and have explored the narrative structure of familiar stories. This type of prediction may also be encouraged through the questions you ask the children.

- **Guessing:** Sometimes guessing can be considered as inferior to predicting, as predicting is usually based on a degree of background knowledge and understanding. However, guessing is a key listening skill that is usually associated with a situation when the listener has no preconceived idea as to what the next event or situation may be. In this situation, the listener is actively engaging with the speaker, often using their own imaginative experiences to make meaning from what they are hearing.

- **Reflection:** Reflective listening has two strands. The first is reflecting on what the speaker is saying with the purpose of analysing their point of view and supporting them. For this, the listener would also need to empathise with the speaker by understanding their thought processes. In this role, the listener helps the speaker to understand what they are saying and the meaning they are imparting – a technique often used in counselling.

  The second strand relates to the teacher-child relationship, where the listener reflects on what has been said in order to learn something new. For example, in a guided reading session the children may be focusing on the front cover of a picture book and being asked to respond to it by commenting and reflecting on what others say. This is encouraged by using simple opening sentences such as *I see…*, *I think…*, and *I wonder…*.

- **Making connections:** Listening involves making connections between what is being listened to and your own life, knowledge and experiences. This helps the listener to establish the meaning of what is being heard and to place it in context. Connections can be made across books. For example, a child who is familiar with *Skellig* by David Almond will be making connections if their teacher reads the prequel *My Name is Mina* to them. In Almond's second title, we find out much more about the mysterious nature of Mina, a character who first appeared in *Skellig*.

Alternatively, children will be making connections within topics. You may, for instance, be exploring the fate of Thomas Becket who, on 29 December 1170, was murdered in Canterbury Cathedral. While being told the story, children will be making many different connections: some may have seen pictures or visited Canterbury; some may have been in a church or a cathedral; and some may be making connections about the period when Henry II was King of England.

- **Recognising discourse markers:** Discourse markers are words that link words, phrases and sentences to make speech more fluent. In written text they may commonly be identified as words such as *however*, *although* and *nevertheless*. Although in speech, discourse markers may also include *actually*, *so*, *OK*, *right?* and *anyway* – all of which help the speaker to manage the conversation and mark when it changes.

- **Understanding intonation:** Intonation is the 'music' of the English language. It allows the meaning of words to be changed by the speaker depending on how they are spoken. This comes from the fact that English is a stressed language, whereas others such as French and Italian are syllabic languages where each syllable has equal importance. In English, we give intonation and stress to some words whereas others are spoken quickly. For example, consider the following two sentences:

Cinderella can go to the ball.
Cinderella can't go to the ball.

If you speak both sentences out loud you may find that you place more stress on the word *can't* in order to emphasise it for the listener. The stress can also affect the meaning and the message for the listener. Consider this example where the stress is given to the word in bold.

I'm *not going.*
I'm ***not*** *going.*
I'm not ***going****.*

It is clear that the meaning changes depending on where the stress is placed. In the first line we know that the emphasis implies that I'm not going but you might be. The second sentence is showing that there is no argument about whether I'm going because I'm not. The final sentence actually tells the listener that I'm doing the opposite – I'm staying.

- **Summarising:** This involves the listener's ability to repeat the salient points that have been heard in a concise form. Summarising helps the speaker know if they have been understood and also requires the listener to listen intently, processing the details in their mind, ready to feed back.

- **Identifying relevant and irrelevant points:** The nature of talk means that there will often be information given that is not necessarily important or relevant to the understanding. Think of a time when you have asked for directions and didn't have a pen and paper. The person telling you the way may add in a range of detail, but your mind is focused on understanding and remembering the core points. This is a skill that some children will need to be taught. For example, they need to know that when listening to a story ready to retell, they do not need to remember every detail. Knowledge of narrative structure should help them to store important information in their minds by putting each point into a familiar structure.

- **Understanding inferences:** An inference is an interpretation or a conclusion we make from the information we hear. This is an important skill because there may be situations when what we are listening to is unclear or disjointed. For example, if we are listening to the news on the radio, there might be an interesting story that we want to know about, but as the radio signal is unclear we do not hear all the words. In this case, we would use our inference skills to make sense of the words we do hear

In the same way, you may read your children a story in which a character enters a room, sees blood on the floor, an empty birdcage and a satisfied-looking cat. If asked what happened, the children may say that the cat has eaten the bird. In this instance, they are using inference to draw conclusions and meaning that have not been directly expressed by the speaker.

Why you need to know these facts

- Prediction is a skill that children need to learn and apply across the curriculum and in life. It could be that you are studying the characteristics of a character from a holy book in religious studies and the children predict what action the character might make next. Their forecast will be based on their knowledge and understanding of the context and character traits. In science, children need to develop their skills of prediction to hypothesise the outcome of an experiment.

- Being able to take time and reflect is something that teachers often find difficult to do, due to the ever-changing nature of their work. When successful, however, it is likely that we learn a lot from the process of reflection by looking at a situation from a different perspective and evaluating our actions and decisions. It is, therefore, a key skill to develop when listening. Playing reflective games with the children can help identify the process of reflection and highlight its importance. For example, you could sit your children back to back. Give one child a picture and the other a blank sheet of paper and a pencil. The child with the picture describes the scene, while the other child reflects on what they hear and interprets it into a drawing.

- We encourage children to make connections throughout their school life. While reading, we help them to connect with the characters, settings and events of the story by relating them back to their lives. In writing, we teach children to connect with the reader and write for them. When speaking and listening, we constantly make connections to help both speaker and listener know they are being given attention and are understood.

- Understanding the intonation and stress placed on words is vital to children's understanding of verbal communication. Just listening to the words will not always provide the meaning the speaker is aiming to get across. Children can have a lot of fun thinking of sentences that changing in meaning when read in different ways.

Vocabulary

Discourse marker – words that connect different parts of the conversation to aid fluency, but that may not add to the meaning of what is being said.
Hearing – the sense by which sound is perceived.
Inference – making conclusions based on the evidence you have.
Intonation – the change in tone used when speaking, often to emphasise a point and affect the meaning.
Listening – the absorption of the meanings of words and sentences by the brain.
Listening process – involves hearing, attention, understanding, responding and remembering.

Amazing facts

Although being profoundly deaf from the age of 12, Dame Evelyn Glennie is an international musician and has taught herself to hear with parts of her body other than her ears. She was the first full-time solo percussionist in the world and had the honour of performing at the opening ceremony of the London Olympics on 27 July 2012.

Teaching ideas

- Cooking provides a wealth of opportunities for listening skills to be used for a purpose. Set up a miniature kitchen in the classroom. Depending on school resources and policies you may want to focus on preparing cold foods, such as making sweets with marzipan (fruit pastilles or wine gums wrapped in marzipan, for example) or icing sugar (such as peppermint creams). Tell the children that you will read the instructions out and they need to follow them exactly in order to have the best results. You could ask one of your colleagues to come and judge the final results.

- Give the children a range of pictures depicting different sports, such as football, basketball, swimming, ice hockey, cycling and rugby. Tell them that you are going to read out a description of one of the sports. Once they have predicted what the sport might be, they should hold up the appropriate card.

- There are various activities that support active listening in the classroom. The ideas below could be used or adapted to suit particular age groups.
    - Call out an action for the children to follow, such as *Listen and… point to the ceiling.* You may add multiple actions, such as *Listen and point to the ceiling while smiling.* This can be developed into the game 'Simon says…' so children would need to listen not only to the instruction, but also to whether it is an action (Simon says) they should do or not do.
    - While sharing a story, read a description of one of the characters to the children and challenge them to draw the character using the information you have given them. Then ask the children how the description would change if the character was ten years younger or ten years older. This is an excellent activity to use with character profiles.
    - Read a riddle to the children, such as *I am the beginning of the end, and the end of time and space. I am essential to creation, and I surround every place. What am I?* Children can guess what it might be (the answer is the letter 'e'). For more difficult riddles you could have a choice of answers for children to choose from.

- Choose a piece of instrumental music that is emotive and conjures up images in your mind. Music that depicts emotions, such as fear, unhappiness and solitude, work well for this activity. Tell the children that the music you are about to play depicts the opening scene of a story. Invite them to listen to the music twice before drawing and/or writing what it means to them. This also works well with music from the opening titles of films. Choose a film that is probably unknown to the children (the British Film Institute have an excellent list of suggestions) and play the opening titles without displaying the screen. Can they predict the genre and setting of the film? They could do this through discussion in small groups and then feeding back to the whole class or through drawing the scene while listening to the music.

Effective listening

Subject facts

There are four general types of listening that occur: inactive, selective, active and reflective listening.

Inactive listening

Inactive listening occurs when a person is present, but they are not taking in what is being said. In this case, hearing is taking place but listening is not. You may have experienced this yourself if, for example, you are attending a conference, it is at the end of the day and, although you have taken lots of notes all day, you are now ready to go home. While you are aware of the sounds leaving the lips of the speaker, your brain does not comprehend what is being said in order to make meaning and remember it.

Selective listening

Selective listening involves a filtering process so that you hear what you want to but, more interestingly, also what you expect to. If we are used to hearing the same phrase over and over again, we become accustomed to it and, although some of the words may in time change, we do not recognise the change as we are so used to the original.

Active listening

Active listening is when there is a high level of concentration given to what is being said and the information taken in. Other noises are blocked out as you focus on what is being said and consider its meaning. In this type of listening the listener is non-judgmental and empathetic. The following behaviours are a good indication of this type of listening:

- The listener stops what they have been doing.
- The listener makes good eye contact.
- The listener's body language shows respect for the speaker.
- The listener asks questions for clarification.
- The listener paraphrases what has been said.

Reflective listening

This is one of the most complex types of listening as it is a combination of listening actively and interpreting both what is being said and how it is said. The listener will test their understanding by sometimes adding, first internally and then vocally, to what is being said. Through simple gestures such as nods and affirming sounds it is then clear that the listener empathises with what the speaker is saying. This also cultivates a bond between speaker and listener.

Why you need to know these facts

- Listening is one of the four essential language skills. Together with reading, writing and speaking, it forms the basis of what our children need in order to communicate and make their meaning known. It could be argued that it is the first of the essential language skills and, therefore, deserves a greater prominence in our classrooms.

- Effective listening is essential for children to make connections with the whole of society. It affects how they are perceived, as well as the knowledge they gain. By learning how to effectively listen to others, we are giving our children the skills they need in order to interact, not only at school and with their friends, but also as they grow up and enter the workplace.

- If children explicitly know the different types of listening and their features, they will be able to assess their own listening skills at certain parts of the day and will know what they need to do in order to move towards active and reflective listening. For example, when introducing a new topic to the children, you could pause after a few minutes and, using the features, have a listening check for children to see if they are actively listening to the information. Once children are used to checking their own listening, you can then use the check in group discussions.

Vocabulary

Active listening – listening for meaning and understanding.
Inactive listening – hearing what is being said but not formulating any meaning from it.
Reflective listening – interpreting what is being said and how it is being said in order to make new meaning.
Selective listening – listening to most of what is being said, but predicting what you expect or want to hear.

Amazing facts

The International Listening Association tells us that people listen at a rate of about 125–250 words per minute, but think at about 1000–3000 words per minute.

Teaching ideas

- Ask the children to form a circle in the classroom and initiate a game of 'Chinese whispers'. Think of some words or a phrase that can be passed around the circle. Whisper them to the first child, who then whispers them to the next in the circle, and so on, until they arrive back to you. This activity can be made more difficult by playing it outside or by putting music on in the classroom. Children will then need to concentrate harder on listening to the words whispered to them, while blocking out the background noises.

- Choose a character who the children know. This could be a famous person, a historical figure, a religious figure or a character from a book or television. Devise 20 facts about the character, which start in a general way and progress into more specific details. The children, who could be in teams, must try to be the first to guess who the character might be.

- A game of 'Sound bingo' works well if you are able to compile soundtracks to play to the children. There are various free websites that will let you download a range of sounds. Hand out bingo cards with pictures of the sounds on them, such as a vacuum cleaner, church bell or waterfall. Play the sounds to the children and let them mark each sound off their bingo cards until someone gets a 'full house'.

- Parachute games are excellent for encouraging active listening. With the children holding the parachute, tell them that you will call out a colour. If they have that colour eyes then they need to swap places with someone else with the same colour eyes. There are many variations of the game, such as using letters in children's names, favourite foods, hair length and so on.

- Divide the children into groups and give them maps of the school. Tell them that they need to devise a route around the school that they think will result in them collecting the most sounds. Along the route they need to mark four sound-collection points where they can stand for 30 seconds, collecting as many sounds as they can (they could note them down on an individual whiteboard or a teaching assistant may be able to scribe for them).

- 'Do this, do that' is a fun game in which children need to listen carefully to the instructions and watch the actions. The basic premise of the game is that when you say *Do this* and stand on one leg, for example, children will copy your action. However, when you say *Do that* and raise your arms, they should stay standing on one leg and not raise their arms. Anyone who does the action when you say *Do that* is out. This is an exciting activity that can be speeded up or slowed down depending on the class.

Effective listening

Subject facts

To be able to hear what is being said and listen actively or reflectively on what the speaker is saying is a skill that can be taught and encouraged. By understanding the features of effective listening we can help ourselves become better listeners and then model this for the children we teach.

Maintain good eye contact

Eye contact is vital to effective listening, but is something that some people often find difficult or awkward. Establishing a visual connection indicates to the speaker that you are interested in what they have to say and also shows a degree of trust and respect between the speaker and the listener. To maintain good eye contact, it helps if both people are relaxed – this should avoid either one staring too intently at the other. It sometimes helps to pick one eye to focus on, because switching from left to right may make you look insecure or inattentive.

Concentrate on what is being said

If possible, the listener should remove distractions to be able to actively listen to the speaker. In a classroom situation, it is the teacher's role to ensure the environment and atmosphere is conducive to effective listening. In some cases there may be distractions that are not in the control of the listener or speaker. The skill then comes in keeping the distractions at the periphery of the mind, while concentrating on the meaning of what is being said.

Keep an open mind

It can be tempting to make up your mind about a topic within the first few sentences you hear. This is especially true if the listener already holds very strong opinions about the topic being spoken about, or if they have preconceived ideas about the speaker. However, to listen effectively, the listener must keep an open mind and be prepared to build on their own understanding, possibly adapting or changing their own views.

Ask questions to clarify points

When effectively listening to what someone or a group of people is saying, the listener may have a range of questions to ask. However, it is important first to ask questions that clarify the meaning of what is being said. This gives the speaker the chance to reiterate the point being made and the listener the chance to ascertain the correct meaning. Asking questions to clarify points also indicates to the speaker that you are open to the responses they may have, are really listening and not are prejudging them.

Seek empathy with the speaker

Empathetic listening is the ability to put yourself in another person's shoes with the aim of having a better understanding of that person's emotions or feelings. It does not mean that the listener agrees with the speaker, but just that they aim to see the facts from their point of view. For example, in a role-play situation we may be listening to Henry VIII's predicament about wanting to divorce Anne Boleyn but not being allowed to by the Church of England. We do not need to *agree* with his point of view, but we would try to *empathise* with him. This is important as empathy can help us to understand a particular point of view or reason for an action without actually condoning it.

Listen to non-verbal cues

Statistics vary across different studies, however, it is generally recognised that around seven per cent of our communication is done verbally and 93 per cent is non-verbal. Non-verbal communication consists of facial expressions, posture, hand gestures and tone of voice. To listen effectively, therefore, we need to take all these into account.

Why you need to know these facts

- As our brains work four times the speed that someone can speak, to listen effectively we need to really focus so we do not allow our mind to wander. Understanding explicitly the skills associated with effective listening will help listeners to check themselves to ensure they are listening attentively and reflectively.

- Effective listening can build trust and respect between people, and prevent misunderstandings that can lead to conflict, frustration or hurt feelings. Understanding how to listen and what listening actually is can be a valuable way to support these elements of PSHE within a class or school environment.

- Through effective listening, knowledge can grow and a deeper empathy between listener and speaker can develop.

- An atmosphere of trust is essential to make the classroom environment conducive for learning about effective listening. In this supportive space, children can develop:
  - increased self-esteem
  - an understanding of the shared learning experience
  - trustworthy relationships with their teacher and peers
  - their own ground rules, which are followed by the class
  - increased motivation
  - clear communication skills
  - clarification of their own needs.

- Listening is an integral part of the reading process. It helps to build vocabulary, increase fluency and aid comprehension. Supporting reading through listening enables children to build their skills and access the curriculum at their level.

Vocabulary

Empathy – the ability to understand feelings experienced by another.

Non-verbal cues – forms of wordless communication, such as facial expressions, posture, hand gestures, tone of voice and smell.

Amazing facts

The Chinese characters that make up the verb 'to listen' tell us that listening involves the ears, the eyes, undivided attention and the heart.

Teaching ideas

- Use the 'Silence game' to promote appreciation of the sounds we usually take for granted. This works well if you are able to display a timer on an interactive whiteboard. Set the timer to a range of different times depending on the age and concentration levels of the class or group being taught. Challenge the children to listen carefully to all the sounds they can hear within the time period.

- A fun activity to encourage children to listen and repeat musical patterns is 'Follow the rhythm'. Start simply by clapping a rhythm, which children then repeat. The complexity and speed of the rhythm can then be built up. Children will enjoy the challenge of remembering and repeating the rhythm as well as taking turns to be the rhythm maker. This activity can also be done with rhythmic songs. Scout campfire songs provide great potential, such as the following, which is chanted as a call and response:

  Flea
  Flea fly
  Flea fly flo
  Come-a lata come a lata come-a lata vista
  Oh no no no not the vista
  Vista
  Vista
  Eenie meenie decimeenie oowala wala meenie
  Exameenie sala meenie ooh wala wala meenie
  Beep beadalily oaten boaten boo boe bedoaten dottin

- Many parents may have used the game 'I went to the shops and...' on long car journeys as it has excellent qualities to help children listen attentively, understand, remember and repeat what has been said. Choose a child to start the shopping list by saying *I went to the shops and bought a (banana).* The next child needs to repeat the sentence and then add their product to the shopping list. The game continues until there is a break in the list.

- Rhyming is an excellent way to actively listen to the tune of the words spoken. Choose a performance poem, such as 'Poetics' by Benjamin Zephaniah. The poem, as the first stanza below shows, helps us understand the pleasure of poetry as we find it wherever we look.

There's a poem on your face
There's a poem in the sky
There's a poem in outta space
There are poems passing by,
There are poems in your dreams
There are poems in your head
Sometimes I cannot get to sleep
Cause there are poems in me bed.

Encourage the children to explore the poem and use their imagination to consider other places they may find poems. Working in pairs, invite them to bounce the lines backwards and forwards, listening carefully to the sounds of the words that they need to rhyme.

- To encourage differentiation of words when listening, play 'Odd word out'. Tell the children that they need to listen out for a vegetable (or car, country, fruit, subject, girl's name and so on). When they hear it, they should shout it back.

Tree, bed, pencil, cabbage, paper
Key, cabbage, road, window
School, door, book, lettuce

Vary the speed, pitch and volume of the activity to add to the challenge. Also, you could include some more obscure vegetables, such as arugula, beets or chicory, and then ask children which one from the list they think is the vegetable.

Resources

Recommended further reading

Just Imagine: Music, images and text to inspire creative writing by James Carter (Routledge) is an excellent text with a section focused on using music in the classroom. This helps develop children's listening skills and encourages creative writing.

Speaking and Listening Games by Margaret Curran (Brilliant Publications)

Teach Speaking and Listening in the Primary School by Elizabeth Grugeon, Lorraine Hubbard, Carol Smith and Lyn Dawes (David Fulton)

Recommended children's texts

Skellig by David Almond (Hodder)

My Name is Mina by David Almond (Hodder)

Drama

Chapter 4

The power of drama, enabling children to inhabit places and situations previously unknown to them and allowing access to fictional settings, opens up a wealth of imaginative experiences that can deepen their knowledge and understanding of subjects or themes. This occurs, in part, due to the intellectually and demanding nature of drama, which encourages children to experiment with images in their minds, making them visible and heard, in order to learn something new. On a continuum from formal to informal drama, we will focus on the central area of 'process' or 'classroom drama'.

Classroom drama

Subject facts

The drama continuum

With formal drama encapsulating such facets as formal theatre trips, prepared plays and school shows at one end of the continuum, and informal drama such as playground games at the other end, it is classroom or process drama that takes the central area and will be discussed in this chapter. Classroom drama has language at its heart, encouraging the children to mould their ideas and articulate them in a variety of ways, alongside guidance and support from their teacher. In classroom drama, children will use speaking and listening, alongside a range of dramatic conventions, to deepen their understanding of a character or a situation.

Formal drama	Classroom drama	Informal drama
Theatre trips	Teacher in role	Playground games
Reading scripts	Hot-seating	Role-play area
Prepared plays	Improvisation	Unstructured play
End-of-term productions		

Content and form

Within each dramatic experience there needs to be a balance between the content of the drama and the form. These decisions will be taken by the teacher and the allocation will change depending on the class and the learning expected. In some cases, more emphasis on the form of the drama may be preferred – this might be if children are new to the convention used or if specific questions are to be explored and answered. An emphasis on content may be suitable when the teacher chooses to use a dramatic convention to explore a crucial point in a text, stimulating new learning through the progression and development of the drama.

Tension

To harness the power of drama it is important to identify the engaging force that will draw the children to the heart of the drama, where they will discover new meanings. Tension can help create an environment where children will work outside their comfort zone. While the creation of tension can be premeditated, it often arises in unforeseen instances. When this happens, the teacher will need to seize the moment and utilise the opportunity.

Emotional engagement

Related to tension is the emotional engagement found within texts, stories and themes. When children become emotionally connected to a character, a place or a situation, it will often increase their belief and their need to solve the problem or predicament posed through the drama chosen.

Decision-making

It is likely that there will be some key decisions to be made within the drama. For example, in *The Paperbag Prince* by Colin Thompson, the villagers need to decide how to protest against the dump, which is at the end of their country lane. These decisions should be limited in order for the progression of the drama to be managed skilfully, either by the teacher or the children. Some decisions may be planned, whereas others may arise unexpectedly; a rigid plan could result in predictable responses from the children, so a flexible plan would be preferable to invite responses that take the drama into unexpected and unexplored areas.

Why you need to know these facts

- The drama continuum helps to keep in mind the type of drama used and to understand that there are many forms of drama, each with their own importance and relevance, dependent on the situation. The level of teacher input varies depending on where the drama lies on the continuum, with a greater degree of speaking and listening exploration and development within the classroom drama range.

- Having an understanding of the aspects of content and form enables the teacher to plan the drama's level of focus on either technical features or the exploration of thoughts and ideas.

- Tension and engagement are crucial to any drama. The skill comes in being able to identify these points, not only within specific texts, but also by being able to seize opportune moments within the drama that may have been unforeseen in the planning stage. This skill of 'seizing the moment' has been extensively researched by Teresa Cremin (see the Resources section at the end of this chapter). It is important as, by its very nature, it requires the teacher to be living the drama with the children, and feeling for the opportunities when using drama will further children's understanding.

- Drama enables children to explore and investigate new ideas, thoughts and indeed worlds that were previously unknown to them. The children will need to make difficult decisions that will move the drama forward as well as foster new learning.

Vocabulary

Classroom drama – drama that is focused on the discovery of new knowledge about a character or situation, often involving both the children and the teacher working in role.
Drama content – the learning that takes place within the drama and the themes being explored (such as bullying or prejudice).
Drama continuum – a spectrum showing the nature of drama, ranging from informal to formal drama conventions.
Drama form – the technical conventions used in a drama, such as hot-seating.
Emotional engagement – to connect to the drama either through personal experience or empathy.
Seize the moment – to use unplanned drama in direct response to the children's interactions to further develop their understanding.

Common misconceptions

Rather than 'doing drama' as a one-off event, it should be considered to be a key tool used as part of everyday teaching, helping to generate new insights across all themes, topics and subjects.

Teaching ideas

These teaching ideas can be used as drama games to encourage speaking and listening in the classroom and as warm-ups to using various drama conventions.

- Opportunities to 'seize the moment' often present themselves in highly emotive texts. For example, in the powerful book *The Savage* by David Almond we are moved by the situation Blue Baker finds himself in. We find out early on that Blue's father has died and that Blue is being bullied at school. David Almond draws us into the situation superbly describing the playground taunts that cause Blue to break down. Depending on the class and the context, this could be a moment of high emotion where the scene could be frozen to explore Blue's feelings, the bully's feelings and those of the onlookers.

- On sticky notes, write the names of real or fictional characters that the children are familiar with and that are suitable for their age – for example, Matilda, the Gruffalo or the Big Bad Wolf. Without looking at the names, ask the children to stick the notes on their backs and then ask each other questions to find out who their character is. You could set them the extra challenge of finding out in fewer than five or ten questions. Talk about the types of questions they used and evaluate how effective they were, before playing the game again with a new set of names.

- As a hot-seating exercise, ask one of the children to be an expert 'professor' on a particular subject. It works well if the subjects chosen are quite abstract so the child can make up the information from their imagination. Welcome the professor into the classroom to sit on the 'hot-seat' and introduce them to build a sense of anticipation. Then invite the other children to ask them questions about their subject specialism.

- Organise the children into pairs, ready for a game of 'Word ping-pong'. This is a great way to encourage fast thinking and to extend sentences. Invite two children to play ping-pong, but instead of using a bat and ball they will be using words. The first child serves with a word from the display wall or one given by the teacher, such as *cautiously*. The second child bats back with a word that could continue the sentence, such as *she*. The game continues until either there is a pause or a word is used that does not fit. The game can be extended into a storytelling exercise by briefing each pair with a set of characters and settings from which to work.

Freeze-frame

Subject facts

Freeze-frames are used to stop the action in a text or event, or possibly to depict a memory, dream, photograph or emotion. The children use their bodies to create a still image. Freeze-frames can be brought to life to move the action on and then frozen again. At any point, the inner thoughts of the characters can be voiced simply by the teacher touching the shoulder of a child.

Setting up freeze-frames

It is important that children know the routine when freeze-frames are used within the classroom. The teacher may give thinking time by, for example, saying: *I'm going to ask you to create a freeze-frame showing...* It is useful if children already know their working groups, or are aware of the process of forming working groups quickly, to avoid any break in the imaginative process. The freeze-frames work best when children are given a short amount of time to consider their frame, position themselves and freeze. This sense of urgency means that the result is not a 'polished' performance, but reflects initial thoughts that can be shaped and developed throughout the lesson.

Condensing meaning

Freeze-frames require the children to condense the meaning they have made from the text or event they are exploring into a single moment. It works well when depicting highly emotive scenes, such as the moment in *The Wreck of the Zanzibar* by Michael Morpurgo when Laura's brother, Billy, announces that he is leaving home to become a ship's cabin boy.

Talking up

Freeze-frames should be seen as part of the natural progression of the lesson rather than a disjointed break from 'normal' proceedings. One way to help ensure a seamless transition is by 'talking up' to the freeze-frame. Give children a short amount of time to decide on and then freeze their frame (a reminder of the context and significance of the moment is important at this stage). For example, if producing a freeze-frame of the moment Howard Carter and his archaeologists walked into the tomb of Tutankhamun, the teacher counts down from five to zero to indicate the moment when all frames should be still and silent. Then they 'talk up' to the moment the children reveal the thoughts and feelings of the characters in the frames. So the teacher might say: *Lead by Howard Carter, the group eagerly entered the tomb. Looking around, their breath was taken away by what was in front of them. Carter was not able to withhold his sense of excitement, pride and achievement saying...* At this point the teacher touches a child on the shoulder, a sign already confirmed as the invitation for the child to speak their thoughts in role.

Choosing suitable moments

Children can be taught the routine of creating freeze-frames and will soon become proficient in entering into this drama convention. But, however skilful the children are, they will only be able to create an effective freeze-frame if the teacher has chosen an appropriate point where significant meaning can be embodied. Moments that encompass tension, emotion or choice will engage the children and give them a real purpose and a sense of meaning to the drama, as they know that this is a turning point for a character or situation.

Why you need to know these facts

- Freeze-frames promote imaginative contexts that lend themselves to a wide range of oral responses. While discussing and evaluating freeze-frames, children will spontaneously be involved in discussing, listening and formulating ideas together. They will instinctively adapt their speech, as well as their facial expressions and gestures, depending on the role they are in.

- It is important that the freeze-frame convention does not become a hindrance to the learning taking place. This could occur if the 'teaching' of the freeze-frame becomes a focal point or the time children have to discuss and generate ideas is extended. It should not be the lesson focus, but just one of many teaching tools that can be used to extend children's experiences and learning through dialogue, discussion and disseminating ideas.

- Talking up to a freeze-frame or any drama convention enables the teacher to create the mood and atmosphere needed. It is likely that there will be a buzz of excitement, anticipation and rapid sharing of ideas before the teacher counts down to the freeze. The talk up helps to remind the children of the context.

- In order for the freeze-frames to be meaningful and relevant, the choice of the moment is important. For example, if there is a family photograph being taken, instead of simply asking the children to represent that picture, suggest that there is one member of the family who is holding a dark secret.

Vocabulary

Freeze-frame – depicting an instance in a story or event as a frozen moment in time (also 'tableaux', 'still image' or 'statue-making').
Talking up – moving away from the text and narrating the events leading up to the freeze-frame.

Amazing facts

In the medium of film, director George Roy Hill frequently made use of freeze-frames when depicting the death of a character. A famous example is from the end of the classic western *Butch Cassidy and the Sundance Kid* when the pair run to their deaths at the hands of the Bolivian forces. Their deaths are inevitable so the scene freezes, leaving the prediction to the audience.

Common misconceptions

A freeze-frame is often seen as a one-off event, which once created is left in limbo. However, it is important that it is moulded into the lesson, perhaps with the use of music or by juxtaposing it with a reading or part of the narrative.

Teaching ideas

Freeze-frames lend themselves across the curriculum so the ideas below can easily be adapted to other texts, subjects and themes.

- Choose a book or a theme that lends itself to a sense of intrigue. For example, in *The Watertower* by Gary Crew the two main characters are warned against venturing up to the watertower. The reader is intrigued why this would be, so many questions of possibility can be generated. Going against this advice, the characters arrive at the outer area of the tower only to find that the security fence is flattened and lies twisted on the ground. Consider with the children why this may have happened. Keep the sense of mystery alive by using words of possibility, such as *maybe*, *possibly*, *could have* and *might have*. After collecting some ideas, invite the children to create a freeze-frame of the moment the fence came down. When sharing their frame, ask the children to think of a caption to accompany it. Encourage them to think of captions that will continue to intrigue the reader.

- Invite children to take on the role of an undercover journalist looking for the story or photo that will make them famous. There are endless opportunities to use this across the curriculum, such as a photo of when the War Cabinet decided that war should be declared in World War II, or the scene on *HMS Victory* when Nelson is shot, or the moment that the 2012 Olympic Games were awarded to London. Once freeze-frames have been generated, focus on the internal thoughts and feelings of the characters involved, touching a child on the shoulder to invite them to share their thoughts while in role.

Hot-seating

Subject facts

In this powerful dramatic convention, members of the class and/or the teacher assume the role of one or more characters and are questioned by the rest of the class to explore their motives, attitudes and actions.

Who is in the hot-seat?

It is often useful if the teacher or an assistant joins one or two of the children in the 'hot-seat', helping to guide answers when needed and providing prompts if any children find the role difficult. For this reason, it would not be unusual for there to be three or four people assuming the role of one character. It also provides an opportunity for language development by answering some of the questions with your own question, such as *Well, what would you have done in my position?*

Be aware that there can be difficulties if the children is unfamiliar with the role or does not have enough information. For example, if the role is a historical figure and the child is ill-prepared, the hot-seating experience may become uncomfortable and the information gained will lack in substance.

Tension and challenge

A sense of tension or challenge is important for there to be purpose to the hot-seating exercise. This could be built up beforehand using freeze-frames or interior monologue, where identifying a relevant moment is vital. For example, in *The Rainbow Fish* by Marcus Pfister the Rainbow Fish has not got any friends because he will not share his scales. The children may be able to relate to this situation through personal experience or through the shared experiences of other children in the class. In this way, it holds a challenging emotional connection for the children, which could be investigated further using the hot-seating method.

Questioners' role

The rest of the class can be given roles so their questions will be directed from a particular point of view. This offers the opportunity for conflicting questions, depending on the role adopted. For example, in the text *Rose Meets Mr Wintergarten* by Bob Graham there is a superb opportunity to hot-seat the mysterious Mr Wintergarten when he comes out of his house and sits on the doorstep. Working in groups, the children take on different roles, such as the local horticultural society (his garden was a mess!), the neighbourhood watch, the local newspaper and the church congregation. They can then ask relevant questions from the perspective of their character using what their character would know and understand about Mr Wintergarten.

Hot-seating, not acting

When hot-seating, the children are not acting out a role – it is part of classroom drama not formal drama. Instead they are demonstrating the behaviour and attitudes of the character through the way they answer questions, if they pause before giving an answer, or through the emotion they show on their face. Affecting an accent or 'putting on' a voice while in the hot-seat, however, is not necessary.

Time to think

The actual questions are important as they have the power to probe the character in the hot-seat and find out information previously unknown. They can open up new insights and take the drama into new dimensions. Therefore, it is important to give children time to think of their questions. If they are in groups, encourage them to decide on the aim of their questioning before ranking their questions so they ask the most suitable ones first. Teaching could focus on the effect of different types of questions, such as open-ended and closed questions with younger children, moving onto empathetic questions with older children.

Transition periods

There should be a clear indication of the times when children change from the everyday reality to the fictional reality and vice versa. This could be by means of ringing a chime or by the teacher talking up (see the section on Freeze-frames) to the moment the children go into role.

Evaluation

Evaluating the hot-seating experience afterwards gives an opportunity for the class to explore what they have discovered and learned about the character, out of role. Discussions should encapsulate the salient points from the drama and enable children to reflect on the new information, possibly posing new questions, thoughts and ideas about the character.

Why you need to know these facts

- Hot-seating needs to be well-managed to avoid situations where the questioning skims the surface and the children have not been able to dig deeper into a character's profile. By sitting in the hot seat as 'teacher in role' (TiR), the teacher can manage the situation from within the drama, negotiating and pushing towards a fulfilling and enlightening experience.

- Although it is not always necessary for the questioners to be in role, it is a useful strategy that helps explore a character from different perspectives, as well as ensuring targeted questions that have relevance and purpose. Additionally, when the whole class is in role, this becomes a more powerful and exciting exercise, as the children leave their own world momentarily to experience a whole new situation before returning to evaluate what they have discovered.

- The more familiar the children are with hot-seating, the easier and more probing it will become. At first, children may consider it to be a time to act out a character, but this can be avoided through guidance from the teacher.

Vocabulary

Hot-seating – when a person takes on a character's role and answers questions from their perspective.
Teacher in role (TiR) – when the teacher takes on the role of a character to develop learning from within the drama.

Common misconceptions

Children will not be able to successfully answer questions if they are not familiar with the character to be hot-seated. Preparation and familiarity will enable them to answer questions true to the character's personality.

Teaching ideas

Hot-seating lends itself to subjects across the curriculum so the ideas below can easily be adapted to other texts, subjects and themes.

- To introduce the concept of hot-seating, first make an outline of the character to be questioned on a large sheet of paper. Acting as scribe, note down all the things the children *already know* about the character inside the outline, and all the things the children *want to know* about the character outside the outline.

- Choose a moment in a story where the children would like to find out more about a character and read up to that part of the text. For example, in *Holes* by Louis Sachar we are left wondering why the children have to relentlessly dig holes in the vast openness in scorching heat. We may wish to hot-seat Mr Sir, with the questioners in role as reporters, to try to get to the bottom of the situation at Camp Green Lake.

- If you are using the hot-seating convention for the first time, try modelling the convention with you in role as Mr Sir and a classroom assistant in role as a reporter. Before the lesson prepare some demanding and searching questions to be asked. Evaluate the questions with the class, showing how they encouraged full rather than monosyllabic answers. Then let the children take on the roles themselves.

- After hot-seating, if the impression of the character is either not clear or has not been fully shared with the children, invite them to draw their own depiction of what the character may look like, linking to what they have found out from the hot-seating exercise. This picture could then be used on a wanted poster or as the main image on the front page of the local newspaper.

Thought-tracking

Subject facts

In this dramatic convention, the private thoughts and the inner voice of characters are shared publicly. Children will be thinking out loud as a character at a thought-provoking point in a story or scene. There are many ways of achieving this, often in conjunction with another convention. For example, during a freeze-frame it may be pertinent to explore the thoughts and feelings of a particular character.

Empathy

Thought-tracking is an excellent convention to develop the skills of empathy, helping children to understand and consider another view or stance. It has the power to open up new insights and can help to focus thinking in particular areas. For example, *Memorial* by Gary Crew could be used as part of history topics relating to war or geography topics relating to progress and development. The scene can be paused as the war veteran stands, looks at the tree planted when the soldiers returned from the war in 1918, reminisces about his soldier days and reflects on the council dilemma of whether to take the tree down due to development. It is a poignant and reflective moment in the book where the internal voice of Old Pa will uncover insights into the pride, joy and heartache he went through, and we will be able to hear the inner stories that he has never been able or willing to share out loud with anyone.

Cognitive and affective stages

The empathetic process is crucial when engaging in thought-tracking. There are two components: the cognitive stage relates to the understanding of someone else's feelings. For example, we would work to understand how Old Pa would feel knowing the memorial tree may be cut down. However, crucially, the affective stage is concerned with the desire to help the character and take action to lessen the perceived distress. So, firstly we understand Old Pa's feelings, but then also have a desire to solve the problem for him. In this later stage we may, for example, confront the council in a letter or in person to make it aware of the distress and look for an alternative solution to the problem.

Finding a challenge

This dramatic convention works well in situations where characters face a challenge or a problem. It could be that a character is having an internal struggle, not knowing the best course of action, or they may be trying to convince themselves of something.

Alter ego

Thought-tracking can also be used to show two sets of thoughts that a character may have, voicing contradictory views that leave the character with a dilemma. Sometimes seen as the 'good' and 'bad' voices, it is something we can probably all relate to and have all struggled with at times. Many texts give excellent opportunities to explore this. For example in *The Minpins* by Roald Dahl, Billy is sat looking out across the garden to the forest beyond – a place where his mother has forbidden him to go, calling it 'The Forest of Sin'. However, this is an especially boring day for the usually well-behaved Billy and soon a little voice starts speaking in his ear. In this example, children could be in groups of three, one playing Billy, another playing the voice encouraging Billy to go into the forest and the third playing the voice telling Billy not to disobey his mother.

Parallel tales

Parallel tales are an interesting way to get children to look at a text or situation from a completely different viewpoint. It is a strategy that can be used with well-known stories, decisions or events in history, where the 'traditional' story tells the events decisively and clearly from a character's point of view. The parallel tale is developed when we start to explore the story or event from a different emotional perspective – maybe a character that appeared brave was actually internally experiencing fear and uncertainty?

Objects as symbols

Objects can also be used to represent characters. For example, at a point in your teaching where there is a challenge, problem or tension faced by a character, invite the children to form a circle around an object, such as a chair. The idea is that you 'talk up' to the problem and then children step forward, touch the chair and voice their thoughts in role. Other objects relating to a specific text or situation could be used. For example, children could hold a bear if reading *This is the Bear and the Scary Night* by Sarah Hayes, or a wand or broomstick could be held if you are exploring the thoughts of Harry in any of JK Rowling's series of books about Harry Potter.

Why you need to know these facts

- Empathy is an important skill and there are many dramatic conventions that can be used to develop this. However, the chosen technique needs to match the text or theme being explored. Thought-tracking helps to build the belief in the role, enabling deeper understanding and a degree of reflection on the event.

- To ensure that thought-tracking is not simply an expression of another view it is helpful to consider the cognitive and affective components. Planning this would ensure that once the problem and challenge has been identified we would be working with the children to solve the problem and alleviate the character's distress. This could be through further drama or through writing a letter, a protest, creating music or possibly sculptures.

- There are various forms used for thought-tracking and it is important that the children experience variety so that the convention does not become predictable. Using objects, changing the location where thought-tracking takes place or playing music to create atmosphere can all help the quality of thoughts voiced.

Vocabulary

Alter ego – a person's alternative personality, often depicted through their contrasting internal thoughts when a decision needs to be made.

Teaching ideas

Thought-tracking lends itself to subjects across the curriculum so the ideas below can easily be adapted to other texts, subjects and themes.

- Choose a section in a book or a thought-provoking time from a real or fictional character's life, where a problem or challenge is faced.

  Lead up to that point by exploring the character's motives and situation, and understanding something about both the way they are perceived by others and their own perception of themselves. For example, in the text *The Island* by Armin Greder, which tackles the issues of prejudice, bullying and difference, children could consider the life the people of the island had before the mysterious man arrived. Invite the children, in role, to create the scene a week, a day, an hour or a minute before he arrived, maybe showing laughter, joking, comradeship and unity. Then let them recreate the scene at the exact point he arrived.

  Freeze the scene after counting down from five to zero and invite the children to think out loud together, voicing their thoughts. Some may express surprise and intrigue, others worry and concern, or even openness.

  As the story progresses, the villagers become increasingly sceptical and anxious about the presence of this person and rumours spread about him, causing increased panic on the island. In the classroom, this can be developed by inviting the children, in role as the villagers, to role play the conversations that may be taking place.

  As you read the villagers' various suppositions, choose a group of children to voice the thoughts of the man they are so suspicious about. After each allegation and rumour you read from the text, let the group representing the man respond with his inner thoughts, showing the pain and distress he would be experiencing.

A dramatic point in the text occurs when the man is captured and forced off the island. Recreating this scene provides opportunities to hear the inner thoughts and feelings, both of the captured man and members of the island who, although caught up in the drama, speculation and rumours, have now seen the man's face and are starting to doubt their actions.

Forum theatre

Subject facts

In this dramatic convention a small group are invited, in front of the class, to improvise an important situation, which is then discussed, evaluated, revisited and shaped through comments and reactions from the class. The same situation is then re-enacted, taking into account the advice given.

The drama revisited

Revisiting the drama makes use of the ideas voiced by the class and helps to evaluate a difficult situation, pondering on the outcome of different scenarios. For example, forum theatre can be used to depict how events may unfold when a lie is told at one point in a story. The scene can then be revisited, looking at what would happen if the truth was told. Children can then evaluate the different outcomes and the varying impact on the characters involved. The power is partly in the fact that this convention blurs the barrier between the drama and the audience, as both are of equal importance in shaping the events, as in much classroom drama.

Negotiation skills

This technique, pioneered by the Brazilian Augusto Boal, develops children's negotiation skills and requires them to listen and internally evaluate points of view before responding. Many texts in which a tense or significant moment can be identified can be used, as can real-world events, using themes such as capital punishment, deforestation and animal cruelty.

Listening through problem solving

New levels in listening can be achieved through this dramatic convention, as children will have an interest in the problem-solving aspects of the drama. They will be more inclined to listen in an open, reflective, supportive, sensitive and creative way, because the drama is changing and progressing based on their responses, led by the teacher.

Connecting events

Examining a moment in a story or event in detail using forum theatre helps children to understand the workings of the story by seeing the way that events interconnect and build to give sense and overall meaning to the story.

Variations

Forum theatre is traditionally at the front of the class, but it could also take place in the middle of the room, with the rest of the class forming a circle around. Invite children to stop the action with a predetermined signal and make their suggestions.

Why you need to know these facts

- Revisiting the drama is a powerful experience that can help children see alternative points of view. It also helps them to identify how characters react given different amounts of pressure in different situations. This can be used in PSHE to depict scenes confronting issues such as bullying, stealing, lying and vandalism.

- With the teacher in role (TiR) within the drama, they can aptly shape the drama, enabling situations to become more challenging or alternative avenues to be investigated to promote children's negotiation and listening skills. The teacher can create a tension that will motivate children to listen intently.

- No drama should be seen in isolation, and forum theatre works well to promote children's understanding of cause and effect. If this is explicitly shown and then identified by children, they can then use it to help plan their writing.

Vocabulary

Forum theatre – when the audience revisits an improvised scene, evaluating and shaping different outcomes.

Common misconceptions

Forum theatre is part of classroom drama and should not be seen as a polished performance. No lines need to be learned and acting skills should not be judged. Instead, it is used as a space where a deeper understanding of the characters or event can be moulded.

Teaching ideas

Forum theatre lends itself to subjects across the curriculum so the ideas below can easily be adapted to other texts, subjects and themes.

Improvisation based on real-world dilemmas

- Discuss dilemmas with the children. Ask them to think of dilemmas that characters have come across in stories you have read them; make a note of these on a flipchart. Ask them whether they have experienced any of those dilemmas, if so, which ones? See if the children can add to the list. Choose one of the dilemmas to explore.

For example, it may be that some children have found some money and have faced the dilemma of what to do with it. Invite the children in groups of four to improvise the scene. Decide on the characters in the scene. There could possibly be two friends, a passer-by and a parent.

As children improvise their ideas for how the scene could develop, observe the groups and choose one to share their improvisation with the rest of the class. The only requirement is that it is a group that will listen and respond to advice given.

Arrange the class space and watch the improvisation as a class. At any point, other children can stop the action by saying *Stop!* or clapping their hands. They can then give advice to that character, possibly suggesting that the character may struggle with their conscience for longer and that their facial expression would show the unease of their final decision.

Sometimes in forum theatre, the child who stops the action then takes over the character they wish to explore. This helps to develop different facets of a character and see how they react given a slightly different slant on their character.

Improvisation based on story dilemmas

- Choose a text that has a tense or significant moment. For example, in *Fair's Fair* by Leon Garfield we meet Jackson who, while sitting on a doorstep in the worst part of town on a snowy afternoon, meets a dog who has a key around its neck. There are many activities that can be used to enable the children to become familiar with Jackson and to understand the background of this character.

Read to the point where, after enjoying the food and warmth in the house Jackson found, two ragged, wild-looking men in the room downstairs, waiting for Jackson and his friend Lillipolly. Stop reading at the point where we assume, due to what is said in the text, that the men are thieves looking for the riches they can steal from this grand house.

Discuss with the class the possible scenarios at this point. Use words of possibility to keep the options open, pondering on whether the men could be dangerous and how Jackson and Lillipolly would be feeling. (By this point in the story we would have a good understanding of the nature of Jackson and Lillipolly.)

In groups of four, invite the children to improvise the next scene with two children being the ragged men, one Jackson and the fourth Lillipolly. Choose one group to start the forum theatre with the rest of the class circled around. At any point children can interchange with those in the theatre. For example, a child may call *Stop!* and then say *I think Jackson would be angry at first because he would want to protect the house from these men.* That child would then swap places and the drama would rewind slightly with that child showing a slightly different side to Jackson.

Another child may call *Stop!* and then say *I think one of the men would start moving menacingly towards Jackson and Lillipolly.* They would then swap and the drama would rewind slightly showing that child's depiction and then the resulting actions of the other members of the drama.

This can continue with the children shaping the drama, stopping at any time for the teacher to give advice, change the situation or ask searching and relevant questions, in order to develop the children's responses.

Teacher in role (TiR)

Subject facts

This is possibly the most powerful dramatic convention the teacher has to use. In this, the teacher engages fully from within the drama by taking on various roles. By being in the drama, the teacher is able to support, extend and challenge, leading to deeper and more developed speaking and listening opportunities.

Role signifier

It is useful if you have a signal to show the children you are going into role; this could be as simple as telling the children what you are about to do, before pausing and then assuming that role. Alternatively, you may have a prop that you use, something significant to the character that you wear or hold.

In and out of role

Being in role is powerful, but it is important to be able to come out of role in order to help the class reflect on what has just taken place, to ask questions, to develop the characters, to look at the situation from a different stance and to take advice from the class before assuming the role again. This enables you to manage the role and gives time and space for you and the class to assess and reflect on the drama.

The roles

There is a range of roles you can take within the drama, each with its own social status and power. Within this range there are five predominant roles that are detailed below.

- **The powerful role:** This can, by its very nature, be quite controlling and influential. It could, for example, be a pharaoh or an airline pilot. In some ways it can be seen as a similar status to the teacher and, although it could be a comfortable role to assume, it may not change the child-teacher relationship enough to be fully believable.

- **The opposition role:** This is usually also a position of power, but one that creates problems by opposing another power. It may be used when the wishes of a group of people are opposed for a variety of reasons. Roles could include council members, parents, witches or gang members.

- **The mediating role:** In this role you would be able to see the advantages and disadvantages of both sides of a problem and would be appealing for a common understanding in order to resolve the problem.

- **The vulnerable role:** In this role the character often needs help. They may be at the mercy of another powerful character, whose decisions have affected them adversely. The class will be trying to find solutions for this role, helping them out of a difficult situation. An example could be the stowaway on a ship.

- **The equal role:** In this role, you join the rest of the class in whichever roles they have. You have equal status with the class, facing the same problems and working together for a resolution.

Why you need to know these facts

- It is important that the teacher has the conviction to stay in role and develop the drama. By maintaining concentration and staying in role, the children will value the commitment and the quality of the responses will inevitably increase.

- More effective teaching takes pace when using TiR. Although you may feel 'safer' and more in control when directing the class and encouraging the children to be in role, it is only when you assume a role that children are fully immersed and engaged, seeing your commitment to them and to the drama.

- In effective drama in a fictitious world, children can become deeply and emotionally engaged with the drama. However, when the teacher comes in and out of role, it gives the children a degree of safety, knowing that they can engage fully but the teacher will pause the drama to be reflected upon.

- Understanding the range of roles available gives you the opportunity to assume different characters, depending on the class and situation. It may be that you want the class to take on more responsibility and find possible solutions without relying on you. In that case you may take on the equal role. On the other hand, you may want to challenge the class and encourage them to think beyond simple solutions. You could do this by taking on the powerful or opposition role, blocking any ideas your character did not want.

Vocabulary

Role signifier – a signal used to show the children that you are going to go into role.

Common misconceptions

Teachers often think that this is a difficult convention that requires acting skills and lots of planning. Its very position, at the heart of classroom drama, means this is not true. The TiR becomes interesting to the children and encourages them to focus, listen and engage fully with the lesson.

Teaching ideas

TiR is not simply one set of techniques but can be used in conjunction with all conventions shared in this chapter and also works well across the curriculum.

- A good way to introduce TiR to the class is through hot-seating. Choose a moment in a story or event in which a deeper exploration of the character's thought, beliefs and motives is needed. For example, in *Fair's Fair* by Leon Garfield we are intrigued by Jackson, who we discover early on in the text has no mother or father and sits, holding a steaming pie, on a doorstep in the worst part of town. We have affection towards him and a concern for his welfare, while being intrigued about his background.

  Introduce the hot-seat and explain that you will assume the role of Jackson, taking questions from the class with the aim of finding out a little more about Jackson's background. In role, choose the points where you want to add a sense of mystery or maybe withhold information. This will encourage children towards asking deeper or more searching questions, choosing their vocabulary carefully in order to gain as much information as they can.

- Choose a text that has multiple meanings or opportunities for developing the story, further such as *Blodin the Beast* by Michael Morpurgo. Throughout this text there are various opportunities for the teacher to adopt different roles and extend and challenge children's perceptions from various perspectives.

  Share the front cover of the text with the children. Ask the children to comment on what they see and make predictions on what may happen.

  Read to the point where Blodin the Beast is stalking the land. Explain that in the one untouched village, rumours are rife about the beast, what he has done and what his intensions are. In pairs, invite the children to make up a story about what they have heard about the beast.

  Use a chair to represent a campfire around which the villagers congregate at dusk to share the stories about the beast. Invite children to navigate their way around the area, sharing snippets of their stories – stories that strike fear into those that hear them!

At an opportune moment, while the storytelling is taking place, arrive in role as a slave who has escaped from the beast. Look dishevelled and beg for food and water. Warn the villagers that you believe the beast is on his way to the village. Tell them that you know things about the beast that no one else knows.

Move in and out of role at pertinent moments to encourage detailed listening when you are telling, as a storyteller, what you know about the beast and encourage probing questions so all the information can be elicited.

Decision alley

Subject facts

This drama convention, sometimes called 'conscience alley' or 'corridor', is used when there are different choices to be made that could result in conflicting interests or dilemmas. Two lines of children face each other, the character with the dilemma walks down between the lines, listening to the pros and cons, which are voiced by the lines of children.

Crucial decisions

In all dramas there will be a number of decisions to be made, some of them crucial to the development of the drama or story. Decision alley is best used for the crucial decisions, where it is imperative to hear the conflicting thoughts of the selected character and where the outcome is not predetermined.

Developing dialogue

The fact that the decision needs to be crucial and is not predetermined means that space needs to be given for good quality speaking and listening to develop. Over-planning could stifle this process, so instead the teacher needs to be open enough to allow the drama to develop, dependent on the outcome of the decision made.

Focused listening

It is maybe the case that children will have the same idea to share in the decision alley. For example, in *Death in a Nut* by Eric Maddern, Jack is faced with the dilemma of freeing Old Man Death from his incarceration in the nut, knowing that things will start to die again, including people he loves. In a decision alley, a child may speak the conscience of Jack saying: *Don't set him free, you can spend all your time with your mother.*

Encourage the children to listen carefully to the other voices and be prepared to adapt previous voices in order to develop the thinking of the character. So a child further down the line who had a similar thought may develop the point to: *You love your mother dearly and she has always been there for you; by letting death out, it won't be long until you lose her as well.*

Variations

It may be useful to ask the children to spread themselves around the room rather than standing in lines. The character with the decision to make can then move around the room listening to the voices. This may be particularly appropriate when depicting the confused state of mind the character may be in.

Why you need to know these facts

- There is a tendency within drama to plan each phase, partly because of both the teacher's and children's desire to remain within their comfort zone. This can, at times, be necessary but in most drama conventions there needs to be space to develop the situation and prompt the dialogue to expand the meaning within the drama.

- If the character's decision focused on is not critical to the drama, the impact of this decision is lessened and the importance of this convention can be lost. So if the outcome does not matter or does not affect the trajectory of the lesson, then it is probably not suitable to use decision alley at that specific point.

- Discussing specific active listening techniques with the class beforehand will help the children to focus on what is being said, resulting in them moulding and shaping their own thoughts, rather then the decision alley becoming a repetitive recount of two arguments.

Vocabulary

Decision alley – a convention used to investigate the different choices that a character who is wrestling with their conscience over a decision may be experiencing (also 'conscience alley').

Teaching ideas

Decision alley lends itself to subjects across the curriculum so the ideas below can easily be adapted to other texts, subjects and themes.

- Select a point in a story or event where a difficult decision needs to be made. This could be part of PSHE, dealing with issues of loneliness, bullying, anger or rejection, or part of history, looking at a pivotal decision made by a famous character, or part of geography, deciding on the best route for a new motorway.

  Ensure the children have the background information necessary by working around the subject or, if within a text, using other activities and drama conventions leading up to the crucial decision.

  Organise the children into two lines. It does not matter on order or position – there does not necessarily need to be a line of 'arguments for' and a line of 'arguments against'. Instead, the decision alley will reflect the weight of support or lack of it from the class.

  After recapping the situation, ask one child in role as the character with the dilemma to walk slowly down the alley and listen carefully to the range of views expressed. Once they have reached the end of the alley, ask them to decide on the character's decision, based on what they have just heard. They should explain their choice and the reasons why, if possible giving examples from the alley that swayed their mind.

  Develop the lesson from the decision that has been made. It may result in group discussions, a video message or a form of writing, such as a newspaper report or diary entry.

Resources

Recommended further reading

Jumpstart! Drama: Games and activities for ages 5–11 by Teresa Cremin, Roger McDonald, Emma Goff and Louise Blakemore (David Fulton)

This title provides the reader with drama activities relating to over 80 children's books. Clear explanations are provided of each drama convention as well as advice for role-play areas.

The following three texts are a must for every primary teacher. Written by experts in their fields using hands-on research and experiences from a wide range of classroom practice, they provide a wealth of ideas that can be applied across the curriculum.

Creative Activities for Plot, Character and Setting Ages 5–7 by Teresa Grainger, Kathy Goouch and Andrew Lambirth (Scholastic)

Creative Activities for Plot, Character and Setting Ages 7–9 by Teresa Grainger, Kathy Goouch and Andrew Lambirth (Scholastic)

Creative Activities for Plot, Character and Setting Ages 9–11 by Teresa Grainger, Kathy Goouch and Andrew Lambirth (Scholastic)

(Please note, that the *Creative Activities for Plot, Character and Setting* series is out of print, but is still available from some libraries and online book shops.)

Teaching Drama in Primary and Secondary Schools: An integrated approach by Michael Fleming (David Fulton)

Beginning Drama 4–11 by Joe Winston and Miles Tandy (David Fulton)

Speaking and Listening Through Drama 7–11 by Francis Prendiville and Nigel Toye (Sage Publications)

Recommended children's texts

Click Clack Moo: Cows that type by Doreen Cronin (Simon and Schuster)

The Minpins by Roald Dahl (Puffin)

Blodin the Beast by Michael Morpurgo (Frances Lincoln)

'The Giant's Necklace' by Michael Morpurgo in *The White Horse of Zennor* (Mammoth)

Rose Meets Mr Wintergarten by Bob Graham (Walker Books)

Fair's Fair by Leon Garfield (Hodder Wayland)
The Savage by David Almond (Walker Books)
The Paperbag Prince by Colin Thompson (Red Fox)
The Wreck of the Zanzibar by Michael Morpurgo (Egmont Books)
The Watertower by Gary Crew (Crocodile Books)
The Rainbow Fish by Marcus Pfister (North-South Books)
Holes by Louis Sachar (Bloomsbury)
Memorial by Gary Crew (Orchard)
This is the Bear and the Scary Night by Sarah Hayes (Walker Books)
The Island by Armin Greder (Allen & Unwin)
Death in a Nut by Eric Maddern (Frances Lincoln)

Chapter 5

Group discussion across the curriculum

Group discussions in the classroom not only provide excellent opportunities for children to share, debate and learn from each other, but also give the teacher pertinent assessment opportunities in areas that other forms of recording may not allow. There are many forms the discussions could take place across the curriculum, which are outlined in this chapter.

Organising discussion across the curriculum

Subject facts

Think-pair-share

First developed by Professor Frank Lyman at the University of Maryland in 1981, think-pair-share is an excellent discussion strategy to use across the curriculum at primary and beyond. It encourages children to consider different aspects of topics being taught and provides a structure to help them explore and participate. Its purpose is to develop children's thinking and communication skills, leading to new learning. The process could work as follows:

- Within the topic or theme being taught, pose a problem or question for the children to discuss. This could be a question originally posed by the children, which they would like to investigate in more detail, or one that the teacher would like to focus on.

- **Think:** Display the question and give 'think time' for the children to consider their thoughts independently. Supplementary questions or prompts may be needed when using the strategy for the first time.
- **Pair:** Children pair up with their partner to discuss their thoughts. There should be a degree of challenge at this point so that views are not simply accepted. This can be done by pausing their discussion and adding a problem or complication for them to consider.
- **Share:** To create the group discussion, two pairs form a group of four and share their views before feeding back to the rest of the class.

Thought shower

This is a quick strategy that can be used to easily gather the initial thoughts of groups. Sometimes used as a whole-class strategy, it also works well in small groups, giving more children a voice before feeding back to the class. After the initial introduction of a topic, invite the children to call out or write down their shared thoughts about the topic. In some cases this consists of single words or, where relevant, could also include phrases. If written on large sheets of paper, the responses from each group can then be displayed and parallels drawn between them.

Talk cards

The purpose of talk cards is to randomly group children together. They can be used in conjunction with a number of group discussion strategies and the nature of the cards means that multiple changes can be made and multiple groups formed. If the standard discussion group consists of four children, then make sets of cards like the example below.

Use a different background colour for each set of four cards, so if you have eight groups of four children, each group will have their own background colour. Each card in the set should display a different number and shape. Therefore, you can ask the triangles from each group to be the 'envoy' (see below) or you could get the children to form new groups based on the numbers and background colours.

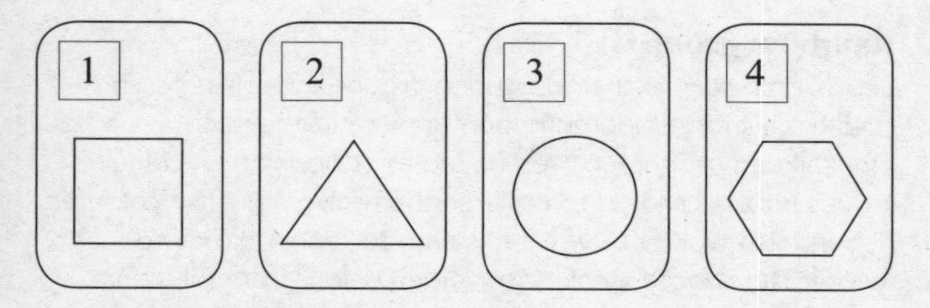

The role of the envoy

Employing an envoy enables knowledge to be shared from one group to the next. After taking part in a group discussion, one member of the group is sent as an envoy to the next group to explain what has been discussed and what has been learned or concluded. The envoy could be chosen by the teacher, the group or be dictated by the talk cards (see above).

Snowball effect

In this convention children first work alone, then form a pair, before getting into groups of four. This then 'snowballs' to eight, before possibly 16 and then the whole class! It helps if a series of complications or challenges are presented to the children as the group snowballs in order to ensure their interest is maintained.

Jigsaw method

This is a structured approach to group discussions that promotes a range of speaking and listening skills. Small groups are formed with typically four children in each group. You could aim for each group to reflect the class profile.

Give each main group a common task, within which there would be a question or a task for each member of the group. These are then distributed among the group through negotiation. From here, expert groups are formed consisting of the children from each main group who have the same question or task. These children then work on what is now a common problem. The idea is that each child will then become an expert in their field. This is achieved through discussion and collaboration.

The main groups reform and the children share their knowledge and findings with each other. The main group is then set a plenary task that draws on the combined wisdom of all the children in the main group in order for it to be fulfilled.

Rainbow groups

Let children start in their discussion groups and ensure each child has a short coloured ribbon (a piece of the rainbow). The children can then be regrouped by choosing new colour groups for the children to organise themselves into. The coloured ribbons also work well when it is time to report back. The teacher can choose a colour (or pick a colour from the rainbow box) and the children with that colour can feed back.

The doughnut circuit

The doughnut circuit is a simple activity that enables the children to have structured conversations with several people in a short space of time; it is particularly suitable for younger children. Sometimes known as 'inside-outside circle', this activity can be used as a development of circle time. Children form two circles, an outer circle and an inner circle. The children in the outer circle face inwards and the children in the inner circle face outwards so that pairs of children are facing each other. Discussion on a topic then takes place before the outer circle moves round one place to the left ready for the next task.

Telephone conversations

In this technique, children form two circles, an outer circle and an inner circle. Facing away from each other, they have a telephone conversation in pairs on the chosen topic. One way to organise this is for the inner circle to be the 'experts' on a topic and the outer circle the researchers. In the telephone conversation the researchers need to gather as much information as they can before the line goes dead.

Feeding back

Skilfully feeding back to children after a discussion can be the difference between a constructive learning experience or just general talk. That is not to say that there is not a time for general talk, when children can discuss without interference from an adult, but the teacher should be aware of opportune moments when modelling or giving constructive feedback can move children's learning and understanding forward. When feeding back it may be useful to ask children to do the following:

- **Clarify**
  Could you clarify the point...?
  How could you have made that point clearer?
  What did you mean when you said...?
  Do you see a difference between point A and point B?
- **Visualise**
  What do you see in your head when you say...?
  What pictures do you see when...?
  Can you visualise the problem?
  Can you visualise a solution?
  Does it remind you of anything else?
- **Summarise**
  What is the most important point you have made?
  Can you think of the common factor in the points you have made?
  If you were to give your ideas a title, what would it be?
  Would anyone like to add anything to the summary?
- **Predict**
  What do you predict will be the result/solution?
  Would anyone like to add anything to the prediction?
  Using what you have heard from the other groups, what could be the next steps?

Why you need to know these facts

- By providing children with thinking time, it will enable them to formulate their ideas first and give them more confidence that what they say is well thought out and an opinion that they will be able to justify.

- Group discussions help children to work outside of their comfort zone as there is a shared responsibility that children sense when working within a group. Challenging children within the safe environment of a group will give them confidence to challenge themselves in their reading and writing, and across the curriculum.

- Children often feel a greater sense of commitment when working in a group. Discussions give a common purpose to the group, within which children can gain a feeling of self-determination and recognition through their contribution.

- Through group discussions you are able to discover what children already know about a topic and so can plan the next steps in their learning. Forming a group gives children the security they need to speak openly and share thoughts and ideas they possibly would not share in a whole-class discussion.

- Group discussions are excellent for developing the ethics of teamwork. Children can build the skills of turn-taking, empathy and working towards a common goal. Explicitly demonstrating listening and speaking skills in the way the discussions are conducted will also enable children to have an understanding of what is expected.

- Children's listening skills are extremely important to help them form and build their own ideas based on their group's discussions. Equally, their talking skills will then be required to share the group's ideas with others, either as a whole class or in subgroups

- Group discussion helps children to think in divergent directions, which in turn lead them to generate more points of discussion that they had not considered before. Children's thinking may be moulded by others as they discuss issues and differing perspectives on a topic.

- Children's analytical skills are honed through group discussion, as they need to consider many different aspects of a topic and then present these points to others for discussion. This is something that can be developed over time, using a range of topics.

Vocabulary

Envoy – a member of a discussion group whose role it is to explain what has been discussed to another group.
Jigsaw method – a group discussion convention where children from a main group disperse into 'expert' subgroups to discuss different parts of a common point before returning to their main

group to share their information.

Snowball effect – a technique to increase the size of the discussion groups by joining different groups together.

Think-pair-share – a discussion strategy in which children have time to think about an issue, problem or topic individually, before discussing it with a partner and then feeding back to a larger group.

Thought shower – a strategy to gather a group's initial thoughts about a topic.

Common misconceptions

People often think that group discussions are most suited for literacy sessions, however group discussions lend themselves superbly across the curriculum.

Teaching ideas

- Use think-pair-share as a problem-solving tool across the curriculum. Set the children a problem to consider. This could be an open-ended or focused question, depending on the class and age group. Examples could include:
  - *Think of three things you know about…*
  - *Consider the definition of…*
  - *What is the difference between…and…?*

Give the children time to think about the problem – for example, *What is the difference between an isosceles and scalene triangle?* In the classroom, display questions to help the children structure their thinking time, such as:

- *What information do you need to solve the problem?*
- *What information do you already have?*
- *What strategies could you use?*
- *What questions will you need to ask?*

After a period of individual thinking time, pair the children up and give them time to talk to their partner about their initial thoughts. Children could be encouraged to test their findings using equipment from the classroom before sharing their discoveries in a larger group, ready to feed back to the whole class.

- Try using the jigsaw method across the curriculum – for example, in maths, it can be used to investigate shapes and their properties. Provide the class with a shape to research and then split them into their main groups, where they each discover the aspect of the shape they will focus on, such as symmetry, tessellation, angles or sides. The children split into their subgroups to investigate their aspect before returning to their main group to share their findings.

- Alternatively, set the children the task to investigate suitable ways to work out a calculation, such as 34 × 12. Then give each member of the main group a specific strategy to use, such as using cubes or counters, a number line, the column method, or their own free choice. In the main groups, the discussion should focus on which method was most efficient and why.

- In science, use this same format to investigate how animals have adapted to their habitats. Give each main group pictures of four animals, such as an elephant, camel, owl and field mouse. Let the children then split into their subgroups, so all the children focusing on elephants would group together. In the subgroups, the discussions should look at how their animal has adapted for the environment they are naturally found in. Finally, ask the children to return to their main groups to share their findings.

- Using the snowball effect is an excellent way to build children's knowledge and understanding. For example, in maths pose a seemingly simple question such as *What can you tell me about one metre?* Encourage children to think of two facts in groups of four, and then four facts in groups of eight. You might award points to the groups who use correct mathematical vocabulary. Other subjects for investigation could include a 'rhombus', '75 per cent', the number '26' or '1.5 litres'.

- In geography, children can build their knowledge of a specific geographical term or feature. The topic could be as open as *What can you tell me about rivers?* Alternatively, it could focus more closely on children's knowledge and understanding by asking them to consider what they know about estuaries.

Through the snowball effect children will be able to discuss and share their ideas and will find themselves searching for the more obscure information they may know. The snowball effect can be an excellent assessment tool if used at both the start of a topic and at the end, showing how children's language and knowledge have developed.

● Try using rainbow groups across the curriculum to encourage children to work with a range of people, sharing the thoughts and ideas of their original group. For example, in history, children could be discussing the positive impact of the Great Fire of London. Each discussion group might consider different aspects, such as:

- buildings originally made from straw were rebuilt using bricks
- the streets became wider
- the effects of the plague were diminished.

Give each child in the groups a coloured ribbon indicating the colour of the subgroup they should form. In the subgroups, encourage them to feed back the discussions that had been taking place in their original group.

Philosophical discussion

Subject facts

The concept of philosophical discussions with children has developed recently with realisation that children are often eager to enter into these discussions, allowing their learning to be expanded through the exploration of ideas. The discussions are based on the premise that all ideas are valued, that 'right' answers are rare, and questioning and open discussions are encouraged. In philosophical discussions, children are encouraged to develop their imagination and ask questions of wonder. These questions could be displayed on a 'wonder wall' (a display in the classroom where children can post questions and thoughts) and then a collective decision is made on which question or questions the class would like to discuss. An outline of how the session might develop could be as follows:

- Discuss the learning objective of the session and revisit the ground rules.
- Provide a stimulus for the discussion. This could be a poem, a picture or an object that will generate discussion.
- Provide children with thinking time to consider what is strange, unusual or interesting about the stimulus.
- Thought-shower questions that could be raised in relation to the stimulus.
- Decide on one of the questions to start the discussion.
- Children discuss the question, building on each others' knowledge, ideas and understanding.
- Draw the discussion to a close and recap on the salient points. Ask the children to work in groups to create a summary sentence.

Philosophical discussions help expand children's learning through the enquiry and exploration of ideas they are involved in. Children soon realise that their ideas are valued and listened to, not only by the teacher or adults in the class, but also by the other class members.

Philosophical discussions encourage children to be able to speak and be listened to in a setting where they are not worried about getting an answer wrong. It is important that the ground rules for the discussions have been considered beforehand in order for the children to feel comfortable.

Throughout all group discussions and philosophical discussions, it is important to reflect on the profile of the children being taught in the class or group. Entering into discussions can be a daunting experience for children who might need structure, encouragement and belief in the importance of what they are saying. Conversely, there may be other children who need to work on their active listening skills and know the times when consideration of others' thoughts and feelings are paramount. Initially, the teacher's use of questioning, and then the children's use of questioning, can effectively encourage further response and comment from the children in group or philosophical discussions. Benjamin Bloom's higher order thinking skills identify six levels of question:

Question type	Characteristics	Examples
Knowledge	Recall or identify information	*Define…, Who…, When…, Where…, Name…, Tell…, List…, How many…*
Comprehension	Understand learned facts	*Explain…, Conclude…, Compare…, Summarise…, Organise…, Describe…, Discuss…*
Application	Apply what has been learned to new situations	*Demonstrate…, Illustrate…, In what ways…, What would happen if…, Interpret…*
Analysis	Take apart information for detailed examination	*Organise…, Why do you support…, What are the causes of…, List the problems with…, Explain…, Question…, Examine…*
Synthesis	Create or invent something, bringing together more than one idea	*Compare…, Create…, Suppose…, Imagine…, Plan…, Propose…, Formulate…, Prepare…, Develop…*
Evaluation	Consider evidence used to support a conclusion	*Judge…, Argue…, Assess…, Choose…, Evaluate…, Select…*

Why you need to know these facts

- Philosophical discussions help to develop children's critical, creative and rigorous thinking as well as their higher order thinking skills. Early acknowledgement and development of these crucial skills can help children become lifelong critical thinkers.

- The ground rules associated with discussions will inevitably help children learn to cooperate with others. Through philosophical discussions, children will constantly reflect on what they are going to say. This is beneficial across the curriculum, as maths, science, history, geography and English all encourage children to consider their own view about a topic or problem, put their forward ideas and reflect on the ideas of others before drawing conclusions.

- Philosophical discussions help children to take time to think about their point of view and the evidence they have to back it up. They will also be encouraged to value the views of others, no matter how divergent they may be from their own views. Respect and negotiation are key values that the discussions encourage, which in turn help the children in all aspects of their schooling and later life.

- These discussions raise children's curiosity and help them focus on important questions that, although sometimes uncomfortable, can form the basis of human interaction. This curiosity allows flexible thinking and in-depth discussions – something the children may not be used to. One outcome of such discussions is that it allows children to gain an understanding of their own knowledge surrounding a subject.

Vocabulary

Philosophy – the rational investigation of the truths and principles of being, knowledge, or conduct.
Philosophy for children (P4C) – a process of critical thinking with children that enhances their self-esteem, speaking, listening and thinking skills.

Amazing facts

The French word *philosophes* is associated with the French thinkers of the Enlightenment period in the 18th century. These were intellectuals who aimed to solve the real problems of the world and wrote in many formats about issues such as religion, art and current affairs.

Teaching ideas

- Discussion ideas should mostly be generated by the children's own questions when exploring a topic. For example, in a recent theme about 'saving the world' children generated the following questions:
  - *Will the sun die?*
  - *Why is the sea level rising?*
  - *Should rainforests be destroyed?*
  - *Is pollution killing us?*
  - *Should recycling be made compulsory?*
  - *Is it wrong to drop litter?*
  - *Should more houses be built?*
  - *Does the ozone really exist?*
  - *Should everyone have an electric car?*

- Other questions and themes that encourage critical and imaginative thinking could include:
  - *How do you know if someone is really your friend?*
  - *Is it ever right to steal?*
  - *If you had a different name would you be a different person?*
  - *Is it ever right to fight?*

- *Should worldwide debt be eradicated?*
- *Can a war be right?*
- *Is one life more valuable than another?*

● Choose a text that raises issues or dilemmas, or which includes images that can provide a stimulus for discussion. For example, show the children the book *The Red Tree* by Shaun Tan. It is a fabulous and thought-provoking book that appeals to the reader in multifaceted ways. The images often draw the reader's eye with a poignancy that can leave a feeling of unease. For this reason, any of the images could be the subject of discussion, as could the meaning of the whole book. If possible, display the images around the room and ask children, using sticky notes, to write and then stick their thoughts under three headings (you could use a different colour sticky note for each category):

- *I know...* (Children write down what they know about the picture.)
- *I think...* (Children write what they think may be happening.)
- *I wonder...* (Children pose their question about the picture.)

The 'wonder' questions can then be shared with the class and written on the flipchart or whiteboard, forming a list for the children to choose from. For example, children might wonder:

- *Does everyone get depressed?*
- *Is there more good than bad in the world?*
- *What is listening?*
- *How can we be friends with someone we don't like?*
- *Is there good in everything?*

Resources

Recommended further reading

But Why?: Developing philosophical thinking in the classroom by Sara Stanley, Stephen Bowkett and Debbie Pullinger (Editor) (Network Educational Press Ltd)

Recommended children's texts

Granpa by John Burningham (Red Fox)
Death in a Nut by Eric Maddern (Frances Lincoln)
Angry Arthur by Hiawyn Oram (Andersen)
The Red Tree by Shaun Tan (Hodder Children's Books)

Glossary

a–e

Active listening – listening for meaning and understanding.
Alter ego – a person's alternative personality, often depicted through their contrasting internal thoughts when a decision needs to be made.

Chronological – arranging or telling events in the order in which they occurred.
Classroom drama – drama that is focused on the discovery of new knowledge about a character or situation, often involving both the children and the teacher working in role.
Connective – words that connect phrases, clauses or individual words.

Decision alley – a convention used to investigate the different choices a character who is wrestling with their conscience over a decision may be experiencing (also 'conscience alley').
Dialogic teaching – teaching that moves children's learning forward.
Discourse marker – words that connect different parts of the conversation to aid fluency, but that may not add to the meaning of what is being said.
Drama content – the learning that takes place within the drama and the themes being explored (such as bullying or prejudice).
Drama continuum – a spectrum showing the nature of drama, ranging from informal to formal drama conventions.
Drama form – the technical conventions used in a drama – for example, hot-seating.

Emotional engagement – to connect to the drama either through personal experience or empathy.

e–l

Envoy – a member of a discussion group whose role it is to explain what has been discussed to another group.
Exploratory talk – talk that explores a theme, developing a greater understanding through the discussion initiated and developed by the teacher and children.

Fable – a fictitious story or tale, intended to instruct some useful truth or to amuse.
Forum theatre – when the audience revisits an improvised scene, evaluating and shaping different outcomes.
Freeze-frame – depicting an instance in a story or event as frozen moment in time (also 'tableaux', 'still image' or 'statue-making').

Ground rules – rules that children feel comfortable with, allowing them to share ideas openly and confidently in the class.

Hearing – the sense by which sound is perceived.
Hot-seating – when a person takes on a character's role and answers questions from their perspective.

Imagery – visually descriptive or figurative language appealing to one or more of the senses.
Inactive listening – hearing what is being said, but not formulating any meaning from it.
Inference – making conclusions based on the evidence you have.
Interthinking – using talk to build on other people's ideas, both constructively and critically.
Intonation – the change in tone used when speaking, often to emphasise a point and affect the meaning.

Jigsaw method – a group discussion convention where children from a main group disperse into 'expert' subgroups to discuss different parts of a common point before returning to their main group to share their information.

Listening – the absorption of the meanings of words and sentences by the brain.

Listening process – involves hearing, attention, understanding, responding and remembering.

Metaphor – a method of describing something by suggesting that it is or has the qualities of something else.
Moral – a lesson that is taught through a fictitious story.

Performance talk – rehearsed and polished talk, often practised for an audience.
Philosophy – the rational investigation of the truths and principles of being, knowledge, or conduct.
Philosophy for children (P4C) – a process of critical thinking with children that enhances their self-esteem, speaking, listening and thinking skills.
Possibility thinking – to consider of a range of alternatives rather than just the existing idea or situation.
Private talk – conversations, usually by means of the internal voice, that are not shared openly.

Reflective listening – interpreting what is being said and how it is being said in order to make new meaning.
Role signifier – a signal used to show the children that you are going to go into role.

Seize the moment – to use unplanned drama in direct response to the children's interactions to further develop their understanding.
Selective listening – listening to most of what is being said, but predicting what you expect or want to hear.
Simile – a figure of speech, comparing one thing with another thing of a different kind, using words such as *as* or *like*.
Snowball effect – a technique to increase the size of the discussion groups by joining different groups together.
Social talk – talk that usually takes place between peers and can be adapted depending on the audience.
Structure – how the characters, progression, events, dilemmas, resolutions and endings are organised together to create a cohesive plot.

Talking up – moving away from the text and narrating the events leading up to the freeze-frame.

Teacher in role (TiR) – when the teacher takes on the role of a character to develop learning from within the drama.

Temporal connective – a connective that links things in time, such as *after this*, *later* and *then*.

Theme – the underlying topic or recurring idea in a story.

Think-pair-share – a discussion strategy in which children have time to think about an issue, problem or topic individually, before discussing it with a partner and then feeding back to a larger group.

Thought shower – a strategy gather a group's initial thoughts about a topic.

Traditional tales – the umbrella term for myths, legends, parables, fables and fairy tales.

Index

ac–dr